BABY
TACTICS

PARENTING TIPS THAT REALLY WORK!

BABY
TACTICS

PARENTING TIPS THAT REALLY WORK!

BARBARA ALBERS HILL

AVERY PUBLISHING GROUP INC.

Garden City Park, New York

Cover designers: Small Kaps
Inside artwork: Widget Design
In-house editor: Bonnie Freid
Typesetters: Coghill Typesetting, Richmond, Virginia

Library of Congress Cataloging-in-Publication Data

Hill, Barbara Albers.
    Baby tactics : parenting tips that really work / Barbara Albers
Hill.
      p. cm.
    Includes bibliographical references.
    ISBN 0-89529-489-3
    1. Infants—United States. 2. Child rearing—United States.
    3. Infants—Development. 4. Infant psychology. I. Title.
    HQ774.H55 1991
    649'.1—dc20   91-24672
                                            CIP

Printed in the United States of America

10 9 8 7 6 5 4 3

Contents

Acknowledgments

I'd like to express my gratitude to my longtime friend Kathy Lawkins Meyerhoff for first suggesting the idea that culminated in *Baby Tactics*, and for her later support and conviction that such a book needed to be written.

In addition, I'm indebted to the many friends, relatives, and professionals upon whose expertise this project was built. I thank them for sharing, through spoken or written word and deed, their experiences and insights into successful parenting.

Special thanks go to pediatrician, educator, and author Stuart M. Copperman, M.D., whose foreword adds a special dimension to the project. Warm thanks also go to Rudy Shur and Bonnie Freid, whose encouragement, patience, and professional guidance made the nuts-and-bolts portion of my work an enlightening rather than a frustrating experience.

I'm grateful to and for my children, Kyle, Bradley, and Emily, everyday life with whom has truly inspired the writing of *Baby Tactics*. And finally, I'd like to thank my husband Kevin for recognizing and respecting the importance of this project, and for his unfailing and motivating excitement and optimism.

Foreword

Having a baby is an adventure. If it's your first baby, you're embarking on a journey through waters you have never before charted. Though there may be buoys, guidelines to help you find your way, you may have difficulty in determining which of many courses offers the smoothest sailing. There is so much for mothers and fathers to know in order to make their parenting a relaxing and pleasurable voyage.

Babies do not come with written instructions. They do have a way, however, of making their needs and demands known loud and strong. There are often times when these demands seem overwhelming. At such times, you might welcome advice and guidance, but you might resent actual interference. This is your journey—your baby—and you do want to do it your way.

Not too many years ago, in the days of extended families living with or near each other, new parents did not lack for a ready source of advice, wanted or not. Though the world has become smaller, it seems families have become separated physically and often detached emotionally. First-time parents suffer the erroneous belief that they are the first in the history of the world to have a particular problem. Then, they either try to muddle through (which is not always a bad choice), put in frantic calls to their pediatricians, or reach out to relatives or well-intentioned friends.

In *Baby Tactics*, Barbara Albers Hill has thrown us a life-preserver. Using contributions from professionals and gifted amateurs (also known as experienced parents), Mrs. Hill has boiled down infant advice into a readily weeded-through and easily absorbed feast. With so many different yet appropriate methods for handling different situations, a new parent can select his or her own menu from a veritable smorgasbord of good alternatives.

In lecturing medical students and residents in pediatrics, I remind them that there is often no one right way to deal with every situation. However, I point out that parents will be coming to them for advice. Therefore, they should pick one method that works and offer that solution. Parents do not want indecisiveness from a physician. On the other hand, one doctor's approach may not suit every parent's personality. Parents should have an opportunity to be exposed to other reasonable choices in order to select what's best for them.

As a parent and as a pediatrician, I have been exposed to nearly all of Mrs. Hill's baby tactics. I've even used many of them on my own three children. (One I never tried is a videotape of a parent working at household chores as a method of decreasing separation anxiety. Then again, my children never confused me with Big Bird or Bert and Ernie.) The methods quoted are generally safe and appropriate, and a significant number of them have seemed to work at one time or another.

Baby Tactics should be required reading for all pediatric house staff in training, especially if they have not yet had their own children from whom to learn. Readers will see that the comments of health care professionals quoted are italicized, and can make note of the name and credentials of that "expert." (These experts became experts, of course, by learning from children and other parents.) The other baby tactics may be considered the advice of well-intentioned friends, neighbors, or relatives. The big advantage of this advice, in book form, is that it need not be accepted, and you need not make apologies nor get into an argument with the advisor.

There are certain basic creeds I believe after over thirty years in pediatrics:

- Child rearing should be fun.
- Parents should be able to laugh more often than they cry.
- Nobody has all the answers when it comes to child rearing.

Baby Tactics is a guide. Certainly, your pediatrician or family physician will be the best source of advice regarding your child's needs. This book, though, by offering choices, may put some of the fun back into child rearing, especially at a time when so many new parents are so eager to do everything "the right way." There often is no one right way. By trying out new ways and finding your own style, by wisely choosing your own baby tactics, and by realizing that you are not alone in facing choices, you should be better able to enjoy your baby's early years.

—*Stuart M. Copperman, M.D., F.A.A.P.*
Merrick, New York.

Preface

Your new baby is no doubt a source of wonder, but hard on the heels of your initial pride and joy comes the sobering realization that this infant depends on you for his very survival. And no matter how "ready" you may have been to take this giant step, the reality of new parenthood is often more overwhelming than any couple may have imagined beforehand.

Time and again, I've been amazed that a helpless, seven-pound bundle can instill in the normally rational adults who are his parents such fear, frustration, and utter frenzy . . . simply by being as unpredictable as a baby is supposed to be. And as he grows, your new charge won't do much to improve your emotional state each time he saves his inconsolable or aggressive best for those moments when you're preoccupied, exhausted, or simply pining for peace and quiet.

I speak from experience when I state that life is no different with second or even third babies, for their needs vary as much as their temperaments. The techniques that may have helped you mold your first baby into a good-natured, compliant soul may meet with complete failure the second time around; in fact, within a week of their initial success, said tactics may no longer work even with baby number one! My rule of thumb is this: When you first notice that a routine is beginning to emerge, you can count on your baby to change things the next day.

The idea of compiling a collection of parenting tips was suggested one summer by a long-time friend as she watched with amusement my simultaneous efforts to eat dinner, chat, and soothe my cranky firstborn. But it really took root five years later, the night my last-resort method of silencing my newest baby's wails was met with utter failure. Approaching the state of dull panic that only too many long nights can bring, I wondered for what seemed like the hundredth time, "What do other people do in this situation?"

Baby Tactics will tell you. I've researched, observed, and interviewed celebrities, child-rearing professionals, and parents from all walks of life, seeking their solutions to the problems of babyhood. With an eye toward the offbeat and unusual, I've chosen their best parenting techniques to share with you.

You will find that each chapter focuses on a different issue of concern to parents of babies, first describing the difficulties you can expect to encounter, then listing those tactics that restored peace and tranquility under similar circumstances in other baby-occupied households. Since babies' actions and reactions undergo a slow but dramatic change during the period from birth to fifteen months of age, chapter information is presented in two separate sections: one for infants, newborn to eight months, and the other for older babies, nine to fifteen months.

Some of these baby tactics defy reason, some present opposite but equally effective approaches to the same problem, and still others may be in direct contrast to the time-honored advice of experts or your own child-rearing philosophy. But referring to this book before parenting crises strike will allow you to "shop" at your leisure for tactics that will work for you, too.

Barbara Albers Hill

A Word About Gender

Your baby is certainly as likely to be a boy as a girl; however, our language does not provide us with a genderless pronoun. To avoid using the awkward "he/she" or the impersonal "it" when referring to your baby, while still giving equal time to both sexes, the masculine pronouns "he," "him," and "his" have been used in odd-numbered chapters while the female "she" and "her" appear in all the rest. This decision has been made in the interest of simplicity and clarity.

1

Sleeping

Sleep is an important issue for parents of infants—and this means ensuring that both baby and parents get the sleep they need! To put an infant down to sleep and help him stay asleep or, for an older baby, to smooth the transition to naptime and bedtime while eliminating middle-of-the-night awakenings, you will need certain baby tactics. This chapter will explain the problem-solving techniques that experts and other parents have used to deal with sleep problems in their own families. Pleasant dreams!

INFANTS (Newborn to 8 Months)

How much and how often does an infant sleep?

Bleary-eyed new parents often wonder just how much sleep they can expect from their newborn. Actually, there's a wide variation from one newborn to another; anywhere from fourteen to twenty hours of sleep in a twenty-four-hour period is considered normal. Even so, the sleep habit seems to elude certain infants altogether—and although a fifteen-minute nap certainly isn't going to refresh either baby or parent, it may be all a sensitive or gassy infant can manage on his own. Then, because he's not well rested, chances are that subsequent naps will be interrupted by the same internal signal that disturbed him the first time.

If this sort of pattern seems to be emerging with your baby, it helps to remember that although most infants sleep frequently, they don't always sleep deeply. They may accumulate eight or so hours of deep, quiet sleep in a day, but much of their time is spent moving back and forth between this phase and a lighter, more active sleep. And sometimes, despite the popular belief that infants divide their time between snoozing, crying, and feeding, a baby may just be awake! Still, despite their seeming restlessness, infants *will* claim whatever sleep they need. (Unfortunately, the same does not hold true for their parents; but acknowledging that this condition is normal and temporary can help reduce it to a mere inconvenience.)

In the early weeks, infants tend to drift off to sleep when they're full and, with luck, will rest almost until the next feeding. Gradually, this pattern will change until about four months of age, when babies begin to associate sleep with fatigue rather than with the contents of their stomachs. A pattern of a morning, an afternoon, and a brief (and temporary) dinnertime nap usually emerges at this point, with most babies continuing to need two daily rest periods until twelve to fifteen months of age.

At night and following a 10 or 11 o'clock feeding, you can hope for your infant to sleep as long as seven hours by the time he reaches eleven pounds. By the end of the third month, many babies sleep nearly ten hours; by the end of the fourth, most have adopted an eleven-hour nightly pattern that they'll stick to for years.

But much as you may anticipate these milestones, and no matter how tightly you have crossed your fingers, there are plenty of exceptions! Even infants who "sleep through" at two weeks of age will sometimes begin to awaken in the wee hours weeks or months later. Fortunately (and to the great relief of exhausted parents who become downright possessive about their own hard-won slumber) many resume their former sleep patterns all by themselves once they're through with the phase of teething/congestion/bad dreams that was disturbing them. If not, or if a sleep pattern doesn't seem to be evolving at all, some of the following suggestions may work well enough to prevent your infant from becoming a night owl!

Getting an Infant to Sleep

♥ We put our daughter to sleep by the clock rather than wait till she became cranky. Even when she seemed to be enjoying herself, she almost always became overstimulated and unable to relax later on.

♥ Our cable-TV service has a channel that plays soft music while listing upcoming programs on a deep blue background. We used to turn on this channel, turn off the lights, and place our baby in front of the screen. Even on cranky days, he'd be soothed into sleep within five minutes.

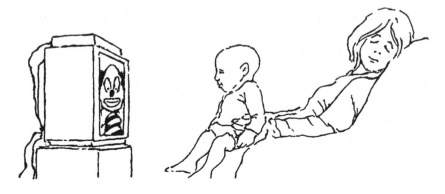

♥   After having to rock our first baby to sleep several times a night until she was almost two, we learned to put our second baby down when she was drowsy but awake. She had no trouble learning to drift off by herself.

♥   *"I figured out this 'football hold' for Jamie that always put her out cold and it's worked with Lindsay and our new baby Sarah. Just give a little jiggle or swing now and then and don't worry about any comments from the older generation on how that's no way to handle a little baby."*

> —Producer Michael Krauss, husband of Joan Lunden, in *Your Newborn Baby* (Warner Books, 1988).

♥   The dark silence of the nursery was too much of a contrast to the brightly lit living room where we'd just fed our son in front of the TV. We had more success giving him his last feeding in a quiet, shadowy room, for he was sleepy instead of wide-eyed when finished.

♥   My baby was always really "wired" by nightfall and wouldn't fall asleep unless I zipped her into the Snugli and took a walk down the block. She'd go to sleep in seconds and, a few minutes later, could be transferred into the cradle for the night.

♥   Our first baby was put to bed eight times a night, because each time he whimpered, we'd scoop him back up again. We let the second one complain a bit and found that a few minutes of crying before sleep helped him relax and sleep longer.

♥   On really bad nights, we'd go for a late-night drive. Sometimes it took as long as a half hour for our son to fall asleep, but once he was out, we didn't hear from him till morning.

♥   *"Aquariums are perfect for a bedroom because their hypnotic calm is sleep inducing, and they make a terrific night-light to boot."*

> —Author Diana S. Greene in *79 Ways to Calm a Crying Baby* (Pocket Books, 1989).

♥ The longer my daughter took to fall asleep, the wilder she became. But the sound of our dehumidifier, which is so loud it drowns out conversation, would magically put her to sleep within fifteen seconds.

♥ I'd lie in a dark room and place my son on my stomach with his ear over my heart. He was calmed by the noise and exaggerated movement of my inhaling and exhaling deeply through pursed lips and would be in a deep sleep within minutes.

♥ Nighttime was one time of day when I didn't mind putting my son to sleep before I put him to bed. I used to feed him, change him, and then pick up the phone and call someone. I'd talk softly and pace, and the baby would fall asleep in my arms.

♥ My son was born in January, and we often found that cold sheets would jar him into alertness the minute we put him down. Placing a heating pad in the bassinet for a few minutes ahead of time solved our problem.

♥ *"Make it clear . . . that the crib is the place to sleep by ensuring that he doesn't sleep elsewhere. Soon he will associate the feel, smell and quietness of his crib with sleep. In time, the crib will trigger 'sleepy' behavior."*
　　　　—Author Ted Ayllon, Ph.D., in *Stopping Baby's Colic* (Perigee Books, 1989).

♥ Our daughter would always fall asleep over her bottle and we'd have to disturb her to change diapers. We learned to talk and play with her first, change her, and then feed her when she began to tire.

Helping an Infant to Stay Asleep

♥ The overhead light disturbs my son's sleep, so I keep a small flashlight on my nightstand for middle-of-the-night checks.

♥   My baby stopped waking up at night when I began putting him to bed in a hat and socks under his sleeper.

♥   Our son slept better when he was packed in on all four sides with rolled blankets and towels.

♥   *"No baby sleeps through the night, only parents do. Even the one- or two-year-old wakes or comes into very light sleep four, five or more times a night. The infant 'sleeps through' only when he can put himself back to sleep. . . ."*

> —Noted pediatrician William A. H. Sammons, M.D., in *The Self-Calmed Baby: A Revolutionary New Approach to Parenting Your Infant* (Little, Brown and Co., 1989).

♥   My daughter was very sensitive to movement. When I put her to sleep on her side, she'd eventually roll three-quarters of the way over to her back and flail around in fright. The first night I put her on her stomach, she began sleeping till morning.

♥   My baby was a real drooler and used to soak the sheet beneath his face. If I shifted his position in the crib and put on an extra blanket when he cried out, he'd go right back to sleep without a feeding.

♥   If our daughter woke up and it wasn't feeding time, we noticed that her eyes would stay closed as if she really wanted to be asleep. We let her fuss for a while, and after that she'd cry out just once or twice and go right back off.

♥   What our baby slept in seemed to make the difference. Metal snaps gave him a rash, plastic snaps left dents on his skin, sleeper cuffs unrolled over his much-needed fingers, and drawstring gowns tangled in his toes. When we put him to sleep in plain thermal underwear, our troubles were over.

♥   I kept my baby beside me at night, so I could hear her slightest stirring. I found that if I nursed her before she became completely awake, she'd drift right back off.

♥   We stopped waking our baby for a 10 P.M. bottle even before he was sleeping through the night and found that by not disturbing him, he actually slept longer. His 2 A.M. and 6 A.M. wake-up calls changed immediately to a much nicer 5:30 and 9:30.

♥   I found that if the baby cried herself to sleep, she'd be awake a short time later crying again. For months, I made sure she was calm and completely relaxed at naptime, even rocking her to sleep if I had to.

♥   *"A pacifier! Mama might as well have suggested arsenic. . . . Lee, who had decided long ago that two and a half hours of sleep per night wasn't enough for a good day's work, agreed with her. 'Why not a pacifier?' he said. He went to the drugstore and bought six."*

  —Author Shirley Leuth, mother of seven, in *Bubble, Bubble, Toil and Trouble* (William Morrow and Co., 1984).

♥   Our daughter slept better when we forced her to give up the pacifier. Before, she would wake up and cry each time it fell out of her mouth and no one got any decent sleep. We had three rough days before she finally found her fist, but the peaceful nights afterward were worth it.

♥   We tried never to hold off our son's naps. Putting him down at the first sign of fatigue helped him get a quieter, refreshing sleep.

♥   Our daughter used to wake up seeming miserable after only forty-five minutes of sleep. The day we started giving her anti-gas drops after each bottle, she began to take two-and-a-half-hour naps.

OLDER BABIES (9 to 15 Months)

Why do some older babies begin having sleep problems?

The period from nine to eighteen months of age brings with it great physical and emotional change, as the barely mobile infant races through the phases of crawling, standing, toddling, walking, and finally running. He spends most of his waking hours practicing these new skills, becoming more self-sufficient with each passing day. But at the same time, his growing awareness of the world brings plenty of insecurity.

At twelve months of age, fully one-quarter of all babies still awaken routinely each night. But even those who had earlier success with sleeping go through several periods of sleep resistance or night waking as they approach toddlerhood. Many become frightened at being alone or at separating from a parent or caregiver to whom they're now quite attached. They may begin to wake from habit if they were offered a feeding or two as a calming device in the middle of the night. Older babies become curious about what's happening in their absence, are confused by the transition from their ever-more-vivid dreams to wakefulness, and, probably most important, begin to realize that they don't have to obey when you announce bedtime!

Naptime can pose a problem, too. The need for naps varies with each child, but anyone younger than a year and a half certainly needs to rest during the day to avoid falling apart by nightfall. The older baby who still sleeps twelve hours each night may get by with a single long nap, while his same-age pal who sleeps only from 9 P.M. to 6 A.M. may not be able to make it through the day without two. At some time early in the second year, nearly all babies' changing sleep needs point them in the direction of that single nap; but you can expect a period when two naps is too many while one is not enough. Until the transition is complete, your baby may seem dauntingly bright-eyed at 9 P.M., may disintegrate at the dinner table, or, used to napping for only forty-five minutes at a time, may simply have trouble staying asleep for the two hours he needs.

Whatever the reason, any time he sleeps too much or too little during the day, you can count on unhappy results at bedtime. You can avoid lulling late-day car rides, 5 P.M. visitors, and dinners that require elaborate preparation; you can reschedule meals; and you can use every winding-down activity you can think of at day's end, and it still may not be enough! If your older baby continues to have problems going to and staying asleep, these more creative ideas may help you:

Putting an Older Baby to Bed

♥ I wait till he's really worn out and then put a pillow and sleeping bag in the corner of our home office. I work, he naps, and we're both happy.

♥ We made a "nap house" from an appliance carton and filled it with pillows and a quilt.

♥ At bedtime, *"Allowing the child to pick out a book for you to read together is very effective. This makes them feel part of it."*

> —Maureen Simington, R.N., head nurse—pediatrics, North Shore University Hospital.

♥ At naptime, I set a kitchen timer and tell my daughter she can get up as soon as the bell rings. It took a few trial runs, but now she dozes off while she waits.

♥ For a few nights, we let him stay up as late as he wanted and preceded bedtime with some cuddling. Then we started shaving off fifteen minutes a night, still following the same routine, till he was in his crib at a decent hour.

♥ My son is confined to the playpen for the last twenty minutes of the day because if those feet as much as touch the floor, he's off and running again.

♥ *"A well-spent day brings happy sleep. . . ."*

> —Leonardo da Vinci in *The Notebooks*, 1508–1518 (*Bartlett's Familiar Quotations*, 1980).

♥   I say I'll come back in ten minutes to check on her, and I do, saying the same words again each time. Eventually she gets bored waiting for me and falls asleep.

♥   His security doll isn't allowed out of the crib during the day. At night, he wants it so much that he *asks* to go to bed.

♥   We use a clock radio to signal bedtime and act as surprised as she is when the music goes on. The battle of wills is automatically eliminated.

♥   My daughter goes to bed willingly as long as I keep her door open and rattle around for a while in the next room. She likes to know I'm nearby.

♥   Our son is allowed to keep some soft toys with him and "play" himself to sleep. (The best part of this is that my husband and I get that extra half hour to ourselves.)

♥   *". . . Develop a bedtime or nap-time ritual to help her wind down and feel secure."*
                    —Columnist Janice T. Gibson, Ed.D., in *Parents*, October 1988.

♥   We spare no expense to make his crib a fun place . . . character pajamas, novelty sheets, musical or light-up animals . . . whatever it takes!

♥   Our son stopped resisting bedtime when we stopped using his crib as punishment for wild behavior during the day.

Helping an Older Baby Through the Night

♥ *"Alexander always slept better if I turned his quilt sideways and tucked it firmly around him under the mattress—acting perhaps as a sort of toddler swaddling. . . ."*

> —British actress and author Jane Asher in *Silent Nights for You and Your Baby* (Dell, 1984).

♥ We turned off the hall light and switched to a night light that projects a picture on the ceiling. This eliminates spooky shadows.

♥ I asked a sympathetic neighbor to put our daughter to bed for a few nights, hoping that the baby would figure it wasn't worth it to call out for me at 1 A.M. (and 3 and 5. . .). It worked!

♥ Once he's asleep, I put a bottle of water and a rag doll in my son's crib. He wakes, sips, babbles to his pal for a minute, and goes right back off.

♥ I think my son is destined to wake at 5 A.M. for life. We finally gave up and timed a little TV to switch on at that ungodly hour. Now we sleep and he watches *Lassie.*

♥ I keep a mat for myself under her crib. If she wakes up too early, I toss a few toys in the crib and doze on her floor till sunup.

♥ *". . . waking may take the form of instant panic . . . if you arrive quickly the drama is usually over in 30 seconds. One glimpse of your familiar figure, one soothing pat and the child is asleep again. But if you don't arrive quickly . . . he may need 15 or even 30 minutes of cuddling and talk before he can settle into sleep again."*

> —Baby-care expert Penelope Leach in *Your Baby and Child* (Alfred A. Knopf, Inc., 1989).

♥ Right or wrong, we take my son into our bed. The stress-free sleep is well worth it!

♥   Our daughter is a climber. Fearing that she might break her neck we wait till she's asleep, lower the crib rail, and put a sleeping bag on the floor. She wakes, changes places, and goes back to sleep by herself.

♥   I bring him an old receiving blanket that I've been sleeping on. It's warm, it smells nice, and he goes right back off.

♥   If my daughter can see anything at all, she thinks it's playtime. I tack opaque fabric over the window glass and pull the shades down over that. With nothing to see, she goes back to sleep.

♥   *"There is no point tiptoeing and whispering around the house . . . you'd only be training the baby to be easily wakened by unexpected sounds. The child who, awake or asleep, is used to ordinary household noise and human voices usually sleeps right through a visit . . . a radio or TV . . . even somebody's coming into the room."*

—Dr. Benjamin Spock in *Baby and Child Care* (Pocket Books, 1976).

♥   We suggested that a particular stuffed squirrel would help him get back to sleep. At first we had to get it for him each night, but now we drop it in his crib when we go to bed and he finds it for himself.

♥   The more tired we tried to make our daughter, the worse her nights were. So for the time being, we let nothing interfere with her nap schedule, lead very quiet lives during the day, and get her to bed by eight.

♥   Our doctor diagnosed sleep apnea, a lull in breathing caused by a closed airway which roused our sleeping baby many times a night. For us, the solution was a sponge ball sewn to the back of her pajamas, which trained her to sleep on her stomach.

2

Crying

A baby's crying becomes a problem to her parents when they realize that a few whimpers often signal the start of an hours-long bout of wailing. All too often, however, those same parents haven't a clue as to the cause of the cries and even less of an idea how to silence them. There are certain baby tactics that have helped specialists and parents before you to calm a howling infant and even avoid such crying jags altogether, or to distract an older baby from a cranky spell and soothe her tears. This chapter provides the best of their solutions to babies' crying. Relish the new-found silence!

INFANTS (Newborn to 8 Months)

How much crying should you expect from an infant?

In the early weeks, crying is an infant's only way of communicating her wishes. And although most parents understand the importance of responding to these cries quickly, by the third week just as many will be rolling their eyes and wondering exactly how much of this racket is normal.

Most newborns can be expected to cry for a total of sixty to ninety minutes daily. During the third week, crying usually begins to escalate, peaking at week six when the baby may howl for three to four hours a day! (Most of this, unfortunately, takes place between the hours of 6 P.M. and midnight.) As the baby gradually learns to babble, smile, and otherwise interact with her parents, her crying should decrease at about the same rate. In most cases, prolonged crying episodes die out altogether by the beginning of the fourth month.

If your baby is a finger, fist, or pacifier sucker, she's likely to be calmed by such activity. Or, if she seems to sleep a great deal, this may be her way of shutting down when she feels overstimulated. In either case, she'll probably cry less than the average baby. But if your infant seems extraordinarily alert or subsists on brief catnaps all day long, she'll probably have trouble winding down in the evening. And until she works out her own calming method, wailing for hours may be the only way she can decompress. (Such episodes will have exactly the opposite effect on the parents' state of mind, however!)

Will your crying infant become spoiled by your holding or rocking her? Will incessant howls lead, as great-grandma suggests, to convulsions, ruptured blood vessels, hernias, or distended navels? Absolutely not! They will, however, let you know when she's hungry, bored, angry, uncomfortable, waking, falling asleep, or simply wishing to be left alone. And, as hard as it may seem to believe when she's shrieking inconsolably into your ear, your comforting presence provides a wonderful sense of security and well-being.

What about colic? It's been determined that colicky crying has a pattern and sound all its own. Despite years of study, no one is really sure why some infants breeze through their first few months with smiles and gurgles while others spend a good part of it red-faced and wailing, with fists clenched and knees drawn up. Some of the older theories suggest food allergies, overstimulation, and a simple need to exercise the lungs as possible causes of colic. More recent ideas include: baby's progesterone deficiency that surfaces as the mother's hormones leave the baby and lasts until she begins to manufacture hormones of her own; breathing irregularities that cause her to awaken from sleep prematurely; or an immature digestive tract that causes her to feel true pain each time gas passes through the bowel. Any one of these theories could explain why colicky crying fades as a baby's system matures; but more important, each concludes that when the baby is healthy and well cared for, this crying is *not* the fault of the parents!

Fortunately, there are a few things you can do while you wait for the colic to pass. Recruit help, seek emotional support, and put some distance between yourself and the noise when you can. Soothing techniques abound, as you're apt to hear from well-meaning friends and relatives. There's swaddling, the swing, car rides, the vacuum as "white noise," and pacifiers dipped in sugar; but in cases of true colic, each remedy will probably only work for a short time. Startled by a new experience, the baby may quiet down long enough to fall asleep, but her wails will surely resume.

The longer and more intense an infant's crying episode, the more difficult she becomes to soothe. So rather than risk adding extra stimulation, it's best for parents to try just one or two calming remedies at a time. While you count the minutes waiting for the delightful, sunny-faced four-month-old who will surely emerge from all this, you might wish to try some of these tactics:

Heading Off an Infant's Daily "Crying Jag"

♥   We tried every formula on the market and finally hit upon a predigested brand which ended our baby's nightly misery.

♥   I direct a fan at some wind chimes whenever she's peaceful. The minutes she fusses, the fan is turned off and her "music" stops. She's already learned that calmness brings a reward.

♥   Our daughter used to cry a lot between 7 and 10 P.M. We learned to park her infant seat by the front window right after her 6:30 feeding, where she'd be completely distracted by the activity on our rather busy street.

♥   *"Immediate first aid for a 'crying jag' involves letting the infant grab both thumbs, gently gripping both [of baby's] forearms with the remaining fingers, and cuddling the arms against the baby's chest. Try it—it really works."*
                    —Pediatrician and Assistant Professor Stuart M. Copperman, M.D.

♥   My neighbor's eleven-year-old takes my baby for a walk every afternoon. I get a break, he gets some air, and he's relaxed and happy when he gets back.

♥   I paid close attention to the weather for months. If my baby was out in the cold or wind, even for a few minutes, he'd be extremely fussy that night. If we stayed home, he was fine.

♥   I can usually avoid our nighttime cranky spells by putting my daughter in a front-facing baby carrier and then going about my business. She likes the movement and the view.

♥   Our neighborhood is pretty noisy, but my baby would sleep all day and then cry for hours at night when it was quiet. Now we leave a radio on in his room, and he seems to like it.

♥   *"When there are frequent episodes of crying which begin during feeding . . . the problem could be severe cramping related to the gastrocolic reflex. [This] can occur in babies with a narrow anal canal, a condition that can be diagnosed and treated by your physician."*

   —Bruce Taubman, M.D., in *Infant Colic* (Bantam Books, 1990).

♥   At the first sign of irritability, we retire to a semi-dark room with a bottle of lotion. There, baby on lap, I massage away his woes.

♥   Her crying seemed worse when I was tense, and I felt the most stress in the late afternoons when it seemed like the day was gone yet nothing had been accomplished. Once my husband took over all the errands, and we learned to live with sandwiches, take-out food, and whatever cleaning and laundry could be accomplished before lunch, I was more relaxed and the baby was a lot happier.

♥   Our baby seems to need a lot of entertainment. When the apartment is quiet and he gets upset, we put him on his back on a blanket and pop a preschoolers' video into the VCR. (Any tape of singing and dancing children will do.)

♥   *"Some babies are tense and jumpy from birth. . . . Noise, tension, bouncing, and any frantic movement is best avoided because it will stir them up."*

   —Dr. Christopher Green in *Dr. Green's Baby Book* (Fawcett Columbine, 1988).

♥   We brewed some fennel tea and fed her a few ounces in place of her water bottle. It seemed to help the gas that was making her so miserable.

♥   We avoided after-dinner crying episodes by putting her to bed for the night at 6:00. She could only last till 3 or 4 A.M. before needing a feeding, but the evening peace and quiet was worth it.

Soothing a Crying Infant

♥   I found a great classical music station on the radio. My son finds the sounds especially soothing when the radio is very close by.

♥   A seat on top of the dishwasher works wonders. The sloshing, churning, and humming calm him right down.

♥   When my son started screaming, I took out an old lava lamp from my college days, propped my baby on his side in a dark room, and put the lamp right next to him. He loved it.

♥   Our doctor prescribed an infant-soothing mechanism for the crib which had the same effect as a car moving at cruising speed. We used it day and night for weeks.

♥   I sit on the edge of a hard chair, feet flat on the floor. Then I lay my crying baby face down across my thighs and swing my knees slowly back and forth. She calms down immediately.

♥   My baby was quieted by the sound of the shower. This worked even better after we bought a clear vinyl curtain so she could watch the water trickling down.

♥   We have a rather large metronome on our piano. I'd start it ticking slowly, place it right in his line of vision, and . . . instant peace!

♥   I sit back in my recliner, put my baby on my shoulder, and slip a hot-water bottle between us. The warmth and the unusual angle seem to calm her down.

♥   We made a Colic Chart, upon which we noted the times and lengths of his crying episodes. This didn't make him cry less, but it helped us realize that his screaming could be predicted and that the episodes *were* gradually becoming shorter.

♥   My wife and I had a pact: while one of us tried to soothe my daughter, the other would disappear for thirty minutes. This way, instead of passing the baby back and forth between two worked-up parents, one of us was always fresh.

♥   *"The things you don't do . . . are as important as the things you do. As a start, then, try less, not more—less stimulation, less intervention, less energy."*

> —William A. H. Sammons, M.D., in *The Self-Calmed Baby: A Revolutionary New Approach to Parenting Your Infant* (Little, Brown and Co., 1989).

♥   We accepted the fact that there was no remedy except time for our son's 8 to 11 P.M. screaming. We'd sit in the den with the lights and TV low, take turns holding him, and watch the clock.

♥   During our son's bout with colic, we appealed to everyone who had ever asked, "Can I do anything to help?" to relieve us for an hour at dinnertime. It was great to get away from the screams, and we came home better equipped to cope with the rest of the night.

♥   My son is fascinated by our canary, which sings like crazy whenever the sun hits his cage. It occurred to us to use the bird as entertainment whenever the baby got cranky. (We even recorded his warbles for use on cloudy days and at night.) We put the birdcage near the baby, turn on the tape, and . . . silence.

♥   I used to sit on the corner of my bed, facing a large mirror, and with my baby on my lap. Then we'd bounce for as long as it took to calm her down. It looked ridiculous, but it worked!

OLDER BABIES (9 to 15 Months)

What might the crying baby be trying to tell you?

Toward the end of the first year, it becomes somewhat easier to determine and eliminate the cause of a baby's crying. At this point, she'll cry less often, for a shorter duration, and for more specific reasons than in early infancy. In fact, her wails will have evolved from general expressions of displeasure to very specific signals that a problem exists.

You'll recognize cries of pain instantly, for they're louder and more frantic than run-of-the-mill complaints. In most cases, they'll continue even after you pick the baby up. Cries of fear will be accompanied by an unmistakably anguished facial expression, just as cries that signal wants and needs will go hand in hand with such gestures as reaching, pointing, headshakes, and upraised arms.

But the most common by far in babies from nine to fifteen months is the whiny, moaning, can't-quite-get-my-engine-started type of cry that you'll quickly learn to associate with frustration, hunger, and fatigue. Its exact cause can easily be determined by a glance at either the clock or the array of playthings strewn in your baby's immediate vicinity; and in most cases your baby can be quieted or the situation avoided altogether by some quick thinking on your part.

If crankiness seems to surface at the same time every day, it's a good idea to plan ahead so that you'll have some intriguing activity at hand. As in the early months, you might wish to offer food; but bear in mind that by rewarding cries in this manner, you may well be setting a trend you'll regret. Another possibility is resolving to simply put aside what you're doing when the cranky behavior sets in, since continued efforts to accomplish anything with a little body clinging to your leg will only aggravate you both. In contrast, giving the baby your complete attention will simultaneously fulfill her need, put an end to her fussing, and bring you some relief.

By the beginning of the second year, you may begin to see signs of early tantrums. Upsetting as they are to witness, tantrums are often a very natural result of a baby's conflict over wishing to do something, yet doubting that she will be able to by herself. While the struggle is in progress, there's really nothing you can do to bring it to a quick end or even to tone it down, but some words of comfort later on can be very reassuring to the unhappy one-year-old. You might try the same keep-out-of-it approach when you hear cries of frustration, for this kind of anger can actually teach a baby persistence if the parent doesn't rush in offering help at every opportunity.

Babies of this age thrive on variety—so while interpreting the meaning of a baby's cries may become easier as the months pass, parents may have to be a bit creative to keep workable solutions coming. Perhaps some of these techniques will help you:

Averting an Older Baby's Cranky Spell

♥ I stash baskets of interesting items (empty containers, junk mail, novelty magnets, an old purse, etc.) near every work area. When my son starts dragging me away from my desk or hanging on my husband's leg when he's tackling a job, we hand him a basket and let him "work" next to us.

♥ When my son's day gets off to a rough start, I keep it from turning disastrous by getting together with a friend who has small children. Playmates bring out a smile every time.

♥ My daughter can handle about an hour of roaming between the toys in her room and the toys in the den. After that, she starts to get a bit wild. So every afternoon, I put her in her highchair, hand her some juice and a few small toys, and turn on Sesame Street. She's entertained, and she winds down at the same time.

♥ *"Help him to learn that not being perfect is OK. One way to do this is by verbally acknowledging mistakes, followed by 'But it's all right because everybody makes mistakes. That's how people learn.'"*

—Author Sandy Jones in "Crying and Colic," American Baby's *Healthy Kids: Birth-3*, Spring/Summer 1990.

♥   We avoid bad moods by spreading a towel on the floor, filling a heavy pot with water, and giving our daughter some toys to splash around with.

♥   My son starts to get cranky when he's bored. To turn things around, we head for my bedroom and spend half an hour sifting through my costume jewelry.

♥   I keep discarded hats, flat shoes, a vest, and a silky scarf in a box on my closet shelf. When I give this to my daughter and settle her in front of a full-length mirror, her smile reappears.

♥   I turn on our electric organ, take my baby in my lap, and let her experiment with the various buttons and keys. She'll sometimes sit for as long as a half hour, and it gives her a chance to relax.

♥   *"If they have demonstrated a set time for being cranky,
start to put them in for a nap a half hour before then. . . ."*

> —Pediatrics Head Nurse Maureen Simington, R.N., North Shore University
> Hospital.

♥   We have a closet in our bathroom with a three-foot by
three-foot by two-foot space below the bottom shelf. For some
reason, my baby loves to sit in there, so when the whining
starts, I prop open the bathroom door, open the closet door,
and let her crawl in.

♥   We avoid the fussies by doing something physical. We
hide, we chase, we bounce a ball, and at the end of a few
minutes, she's ready for anything.

♥   My baby is still very calmed by sucking. When I see
trouble coming, I hand her a juice bottle, and she settles into
her beanbag chair for some R & R.

♥   Before I go to bed each night, I put three or four small toys
in an easy-open lunch box and hide it somewhere in the
house. (I try to pick things he hasn't played with in a while.)
When the demanding behavior starts, I lead him to the hiding
place and he takes over from there. He's very entertained by
hiding, finding, emptying, and refilling the box over and over
again.

♥   *"I sang for her; I danced for her; I made faces at her; I
acted the whole of 'Paolo and Francesca' to her, and she hated
it all. But [regular, sonorous] snoring—from the first faint
sign—she loved it!"*

> —Actress Eleanore Duse, on her experience looking after a year-old baby in
> *2500 Anecdotes for All Occasions*, Edmund Fuller, Ed. (Avenel Books,
> 1980).

♥   We live about three minutes away from a large shopping
mall. Nothing heads off a cranky spell like a relaxed stroll in a
busy place like that.

Stopping an Older Baby's Tears

♥   My daughter falls apart completely by around 4:30 in the afternoon. I've asked—begged—the neighborhood kids to play in my yard after school, and I move her playpen onto the porch so she can watch. Her crying stops immediately.

♥   We're always careful to rule out physical causes by examining her skin for scratches or discolorations and by pressing here and there to check for pain.

♥   *"An elevator ride is a simple way to lift your baby out of his fussy mood . . . the gut-gripping pull of gravitational force is such a novel sensation that it distracts most babies from their woes."*
   —Diana S. Greene in *79 Ways to Calm a Crying Baby* (Pocket Books, 1988).

♥   I scoop him up, carry him to the living room, settle into the rocking chair, and sing silly songs. He loved it as an infant and he loves it just as much now!

♥   Cruel as it may feel, we've learned to turn our backs on anything that looks like a tantrum. Any response at all seems to bring on more of them.

♥   I do something ridiculous like race around the house on all fours making cow noises. His curiosity gets the better of him, and a minute later he'll be mooing right behind me.

♥   I used to look into my son's eyes and say the words "You must remain calm. . . . You must remain calm. . . ." over and over almost like a mantra. He probably responded more to my tone and attentions than the words themselves, but he always stopped crying.

♥   *"Nothing dries sooner than a Tear."*
   —Benjamin Franklin in *Poor Richard's Almanack* (Hallmark Editions, 1967).

♥ No matter what the time of day, I run an inch of water in the tub and plop her in. She forgets her misery in no time.

♥ My baby used to go nuts in the doctor's office. Now, with the doctor's blessing, we bring her doll along. The procedures are done first to the doll, then to me, and finally to my daughter. She still doesn't like it, but at least she no longer screams.

♥ We go someplace, even if it's only to the garage, with my son in the backpack. He can be more easily distracted when he can't see my face.

♥ *"One toy, singled out all day and at night, is a lot more important than a 'whole raft' of unimportant ones. By handing a special one to your baby when she cries for you, you are saying, 'Here, this will help you do it for yourself.'"*

—Noted pediatrician and author T. Berry Brazelton, M.D., in *What Every Baby Knows* (Addison-Wesley, 1987).

♥ I put on some music, put her in the playpen, lie on the rug, and do exercises—vigorous, exaggerated exercises. After a minute or so, she's laughing.

♥ We keep a gel-filled teething ring in the freezer. Chewing it brings a strange sensation and an odd crunchy noise, so no matter what causes our baby's tears, they stop as soon as she begins to gnaw.

♥ I sit him in the highchair and hand him an old billfold stuffed with coupons, photos, old credit cards, and other odds and ends. He's so distracted by all the compartments that he forgets what was making him miserable.

"Yes, my dear. I know how to change a boy's diaper."

3

Bathing, Diapering, and Dressing

New parents are often quite tentative in their handling of a tiny, fragile newborn; and by the time they've gained the confidence necessary to bathe, diaper, and dress him surely and swiftly, the baby has developed some feelings of his own about the subject—most of them negative and nearly all of them noisy! Particular baby tactics have been proven by other parents and baby-care authorities to be effective in eliminating the problems in an infant's or older baby's physical care. This chapter presents the techniques they have used to make bathing, diapering, and dressing a baby simple rather than a struggle, enjoyable rather than exhausting. Enjoy your truce!

INFANTS (Newborn to 8 Months)

How can you expect an infant to react to being bathed, diapered, or dressed?

Keeping an infant clean, dry, and clothed is an ordinary part of a parent's day. And, at first, this may not seem like a particularly difficult job. But the realization quickly dawns that an outfit earmarked for the day may only make it till 9 A.M. before being soaked by a leak, a spill, or an overly energetic burp. In fact, although most infants are pretty vocal about their dislike for being unclothed (and later, when they can roll, about being held in one position in order to achieve that state), four or more clothing changes per day is not unusual.

So, to save dressing time and your infant's disposition, it's probably wise to avoid garments with such troublesome features as snaps or buttons down the back (you'll have to keep turning the baby over), ruffles or bows at the neckline (they'll quickly discolor from saliva and formula), crew- or turtlenecks (he'll hate having them pulled over his head) and legs without snaps (you'll have to undress him completely just to check a diaper). Soft shoes and tie-on booties make adorable accessories, but getting and keeping them on can be a real problem. Functional shoes won't be needed until he's almost ready to walk; socks alone are just fine until then.

And what about diapers? The average newborn will need 8 to 10 diaper changes a day, translating into some 7,000 overall before he's finally through. Of course, this will mean lots more time spent coaxing little limbs in and out of those armholes, legholes, and neckholes, trying to soothe their indignant owner all the while. Experimenting with different diaper brands (or with different folding methods if you're using cloth) may cut down on those leaks that require changing his entire outfit, but cutting corners on the number of diaper changes will only encourage diaper rash. So rather than tussle with a frightened or active infant during those many changes, why not help him enjoy them?

Mobiles, of course, are entertaining during the early months, as is an unusual rattle or toy once he can actually hold things. But even more reassuring is your attention, your touch, and the sound of your voice. Since infants pick up on tension quite easily, you'll both probably be happier if you avoid rushing.

The same is true of bath time. Obviously, the infant who dislikes having his clothing or diaper removed will protest even more vigorously over a bath. After all, he feels most secure when he's warm and wrapped; yet here you are reversing the process completely.

When he's ready for the tub, try a reassuringly small one until he can sit up unaided. If you choose a time of day when he's been recently fed and rested, he's apt to be distracted and eventually entertained by singing, bath toys, and water play.

With the right approach, bathing, diapering, and dressing can provide the perfect opportunity for you and your infant to enjoy one another. Some of the following tactics may help you handle these jobs with more confidence:

Making an Infant's Bath Time a Pleasant Experience

♥   My baby hated to be naked. She liked her baths better when I wrapped her in a towel, lowered her into the water towel and all, and then unwrapped and washed her one part at a time.

♥   Once our son pulled up to his hands and knees, we started bathing him in a face-down "frog" position. He was much easier to handle this way.

♥   I sit on the side of the tub near the drain, facing in, and turn on the water. Then I hold my baby on my lap with one hand and soap and rinse her with the other.

♥   *"You can help alleviate everyone's fears by wearing cotton gloves during the bath. They really give you a better grip and they're a great way to apply soap!"*

> —Joan Lunden in husband Michael Krauss's *Your Newborn Baby* (Warner Books, 1988).

♥   If we let the faucet drip onto a folded washcloth or plastic cup, our son is so entranced by the sight and sound that he forgets why he's really in the bathtub.

♥   My son hates shampoos. We've learned to lay him on his back in an inch of water, washing and rinsing his hair that way.

♥   I used to line the tub bottom with a bath towel before running the water. That way there was no chance of slipping and sliding.

♥   For sponge baths, I undress her only to the waist. Then I wash, dry, and redress that part completely before starting on her bottom half. She stays warmer this way.

♥   We store all the baby's bath toys in a mesh laundry bag, which we hang from the towel bar. When her bath is done, we drape the bag of toys over the side of the tub to drip dry; whoever uses the shower next just pushes the bag out.

♥   We both hated bath time until I invested in a 39¢ jar of bubble water. Now she's learned that the tub isn't always an instrument of torture.

♥   On humid days, a morning bath sometimes wasn't enough. Whenever she woke up feeling clammy, I gave her what I call a "powder bath"—a light, all-over dusting with baby cornstarch. She seemed more comfortable, and she was a lot easier to handle when we weren't sticking together.

♥   *"Invest in a plastic apron or simply plan a change of clothing after baby's bath. Baby's delighted kicking, pushing, splashing, and slapping at the bath water will probably leave you with mixed emotions. . . ."*

—The First Year of Life (Cahners Publishing Company, 1987).

♥   I bought a set of vinyl stick-on pictures large enough to be handled by babies. We bring three or four into the bath each day; and as I wash him, I stick these on the side of the tub, his stomach, and anywhere else he can reach. He's so busy trying to touch them that he forgets to cry.

♥   For shampoos, I hold my baby's head in my hand with his body pinned between my elbow and my waist. Then we go to the sink where I use the spray nozzle and my other hand to wet, lather, and rinse his hair. We're done in seconds.

♥   No matter what the temperature at bath time, my daughter's skin used to get that mottled look that told me she was freezing. Now I cover her midsection with a wet facecloth and continue to pour warm water over the cloth as I wash the rest of her.

Diapering and Dressing the Active or Frightened Infant

♥   Once my baby learned to roll, I found it easier to change her diaper when she was face down. I held her in place with one hand while the other did the wiping and changing.

♥   The nursery is on the second floor but for weeks my son was terrified by the sensation of being carried up and down stairs. We created a second changing station in a corner of the dining room.

♥   *"I found what would make him feel better was to . . . put a warm towel down on the changing table. For newborns it is hospital policy to wrap them in warm towels, so who knows! Maybe it is comforting."*

—Actress and mother Marcy Walker.

♥   We stuck to drawstring gowns and zippered playsuits for a long time, simply because they reduced the dressing process to less than a minute.

♥   I used diapering and dressing as a way to introduce the names of body parts. (Lord knows we were at the changing table often enough—I figured I might as well put the time to good use!)

♥   I bought only front-opening infant clothes so that I could put the undershirt inside the stretchie and slip my baby's arms into both at the same time.

♥   *"Keep something of interest at the changing table that the child does not hear or see at any other time—a tape deck, a changeable wall picture, a toy. . . ."*

—Jean Brandt, director, State University of New York at Farmingdale Child Care Center.

♥   When I finished one diaper change, I laid out everything I'd be needing for the next: diaper face up and flat, powder and wipes box opened and ready to go, etc. This way my baby was actually on the table for only twenty seconds.

♥   Whenever I tried to change her diaper, she rolled all over the place. When I slipped an old puppet on my right hand and had *him* do the work, she lay perfectly still, gazing at him in amazement.

♥   We cut down on the number of dressing ordeals by including a dribble bib as part of every outfit. A soiled bib could be changed in two seconds; without it, she'd have to be completely redressed.

♥ I started out changing my baby before and after each feeding. When I realized he wasn't really bothered by being wet, I cut down on our struggles by changing him just once before putting him down for his nap.

♥ *"Clothing with elasticized waists . . . will soon be left behind as your baby motors along the floor. Overalls or stretch suits protect your baby's knees and stay in place much better than separates."*
—Ellen J. Sackoff in "Dressing Your Baby," *Baby Talk*, April 1990.

♥ We use cloth diapers, but once we began prefolding them and stacking them on the changing table the way people do disposables, the job of diapering went much faster.

♥ I have a night light which projects changing pictures on the ceiling. I keep his room pretty dark anyway, so I direct the light right over where his head will be and switch it on each time I put him down to be changed.

♥ My daughter was standing by six-and-a-half months but couldn't get back down for quite a while longer. I would lower the crib rail, prop her in front of it, and could take all the time I wanted dressing her while she clung to the bars.

OLDER BABIES (9 to 15 Months)

Why do some older babies begin to resist the tub and changing table?

As they move into their second year, many babies who had come to delight in bath time will now begin to resist it. The fact that fears often surface around this time makes the slippery, noisy, confining tub an understandably frightening place. But even babies who aren't afraid are no longer content to sit and gnaw on a toy while being washed. Eager to practice their motor skills, they find that their attempts to stand or climb will be thwarted by safety-conscious parents, or worse, will cause them to slip. And since most older babies dislike being handled or restrained, the bathtub then becomes a place of frustration. If you add to all this the unpleasant feeling of shampoo-water in the eyes and ears (and with a wriggler, that's often unavoidable), it's no wonder bath time starts to take on the characteristics of a wrestling match.

Now is a great time to introduce bath toys, for he'll be momentarily entertained by filling, dumping, squirting, and floating whatever you have on hand. But if his resistance is still strong, you might choose to get into the tub with him, holding him in the safety of your lap while you get the job done. For shampoos, a rubber ring that resembles a hat brim and keeps water off the face and ears is available through many mail-order catalogs.

As the baby becomes more and more mobile, dressing him becomes more of a struggle as well. He's got places to go and things to explore, and he's just not happy about standing still while you fuss over his socks and snappers. There are two benefits to keeping this in mind when you shop for baby clothes: choosing roomy, easy-on outfits will give him more freedom of movement than more elaborate get-ups; in addition, this will cut down on the baby's dressing time. Shoes are now needed; and if you want a pair that slides on easily but won't disappear over the side of the stroller during a trip to the mall, professionally fitted tie shoes are probably a better choice than the more trendy slip-ons.

Parents must now move quickly through a diaper change as well, for the mobile older baby won't lie still long enough for you to fuss and fumble. More than half of babies between eight and fifteen months are prone to diaper rash, however; thus, it's important to change him frequently, no matter how vigorous his protests. He'll undoubtedly prefer to stand, so placing him in front of the TV or a window may distract him for the few minutes you need.

You may reach the conclusion that almost every technique works for a little while, but you'll be bathing, diapering, and dressing your baby for many more months to come. Some of these suggestions may help you along the way:

Bathing a Frightened or Active Older Baby

♥   My baby stands on a towel outside the tub, while I bathe him with its contents. Eventually, curiosity will overcome fear and he'll want to get in.

♥   Our bath tussles ended when I gave her an empty, squeeze-type mustard bottle to play with while I washed her.

♥   My son insisted on sucking soapy water off the washcloth until I started giving him a sipper cup filled with clean water to carry into the tub.

♥   *"If . . . you've got a real screamer on your hands, don't prolong the experience. Bathe your baby quickly and move on to an activity your baby likes."*

> —Nancy Issing, R.N., A.C.C.E., in "Squeaky Clean," *Baby Talk*, May 1990.

♥   I put my older child in the bathtub at the same time. He can help hold the baby, wash her, or distract her as needed.

♥   My son won't sit still for a washcloth, but doesn't mind as much when I wash him with my soapy hand.

♥ *"I give my son a baby doll with hair to play with in the tub. While he gives his baby a bath and shampoos its hair, I get my baby washed and shampooed, too."*

—*Joplin Globe* columnist Marti Attoun.

♥ Our baby is much too active for either her baby tub or our regular bathtub—she climbs out of one and dives around in the other. For now, it's easier to line the kitchen floor with towels and bathe her from a basin.

♥ I have an unframed oval mirror that I put on the tub bottom before running the water. It's unbreakable, distracting, and it keeps her away from the faucets.

♥ We let the shower massage hang down, and we turn it on so there's a fine spray shooting out toward the middle of the tub. My son likes to watch it, but only from the safety of the tub's opposite end. This keeps him confined to a manageable area while he's being washed.

♥ *"You can try a dishpan, but if your baby is afraid of that, give a sponge bath for several months, until the child's courage comes back. Then start with an inch of water . . ."*

—Dr. Benjamin Spock in *Baby and Child Care* (Pocket Books, 1976).

♥ We've given up on baths completely for the moment. Instead, one of us takes her into the shower with us, where she's washed and shampooed in about forty-five seconds.

♥ My son likes the bath part but hates the shampoo part. When I'm ready to wash his hair, I soap his legs over and over till they're almost white. Then, while he's frantically trying to get them to look normal again, I work on his head.

♥ Convincing her to sit on a plastic booster seat helps. We plop it right in the middle of the tub, pretend it's a boat, and achieve two purposes: she feels safe, and she's busy.

♥   Bath time is snack time in our house. I settle him into the water, hand him a cookie, and work fast.

Winning the Battle of Diapering and Dressing

♥   I never made a game out of chasing him—I was always afraid that it would encourage him to flee. No matter how many times he tried to escape, I was very matter-of-fact about bringing him back to the dressing area, pinning him between my knees if I had to.

♥   I put a few toys in a dresser drawer, which is about eighteen inches from the floor. When it's time to dress her, I open the drawer and stand her in front of it. She has something to hold on to and some things to play with.

♥   *"When she's dressing or undressing, allow her to do some of the work herself: Loosen her shoe, then let her pull it off, or put her socks halfway on and let her finish the job."*

—"Kidfile: On Becoming a Toddler," *Parenting* magazine, April 1990.

♥   I stand him on a low, sturdy stool facing me and ask him to hug me while I change his diaper. At least he can't walk away!

♥   My daughter practically lives in sweatsuits. They're durable, go on and off in seconds, and there's no struggling with eight or ten crotch snappers every time she needs a change.

♥   If we dress our baby in two-piece outfits, he pulls his pants and diaper off. Rather than redress him a dozen times a day, we're sticking to overalls for now.

♥   When my baby wears a dress, she's constantly stepping or kneeling on the hem. Tights are a problem, too, because she pulls on the feet until the tights are halfway off. We buy only one-piece playsuits.

♥   *"I've been buying diapers, nearly without interruption, for eight and a half years now. If we'd been using cloth all these years, I would at least have one terrific collection of cleaning rags to show for it all."*

> —Author and columnist Joyce Maynard in *Domestic Affairs: Enduring the Pleasures of Motherhood and Family Life* (Times Books, 1987).

♥   As I put my son down on the changing table, I take a rubber pretzel between my teeth. He grabs it, puts it in his own mouth, passes it back, and then takes it again. It's not the most sanitary game in the world, but by the time he tires of it, we're finished with the real task.

♥   We dress her before she even leaves the crib in the morning. Somehow, she's more cooperative before she's had a chance to run around.

♥   I wait to dress my baby until he's really engrossed in something. Then I bring his clothes, a diaper, and wipes to whichever room he's in and dress him right there.

♥   *"I stopped forcing my babies into high-topped, high-priced, hard-soled shoes the day I saw a 'first birthday portrait' of Nelson Rockefeller's baby . . . barefoot. What's good enough for Happy is good enough for me; from then on, our babies went barefoot till kindergarten time."*

> —Author and mother of ten Teresa Bloomingdale in *I Should Have Seen It Coming When the Rabbit Died* (Doubleday and Co., 1979).

♥   I put on his clothes in exactly the same order, singing exactly the same song about what I'm doing, every time. Knowing what comes next, he's more interested in offering an arm or leg than in running away.

♥   Since no bib on the market can handle my baby's mealtime messes, we eliminated a lot of clothing changes when we started pulling one of my old T-shirts over her outfit before putting her in the highchair. Now she's covered from neck to knees while eating.

4

Feeding

Feeding a baby requires time, patience, and, very often, a repertoire of games, songs, and funny faces designed to distract the little one from the task at hand. To breast-, bottle-, and spoon-feed an infant with efficiency and success, or, for an older baby, to end mealtime battles while encouraging her to begin feeding herself, you will need some dependable baby tactics. This chapter offers some proven suggestions that have helped other parents and child-rearing professionals solve their own babies' feeding problems. Bon appetit!

INFANTS (Newborn to 8 Months)

How much time will be spent on feeding?

Few parents appreciate ahead of time just how much time will be spent feeding an infant. At first, most new babies need to eat every two to four hours around the clock, and the feedings themselves take up much of the time in between.

Breastfed newborns in particular should be fed eight to eleven times in a twenty-four-hour period. At 6:00 A.M., for example, the mother may spend twenty minutes actually feeding her baby; but cuddling, changing, burping, and rocking her often stretches this to forty-five minutes or more. And by 8:15 the baby may be hungry again! The time between feedings usually increases to nearly four hours after a few weeks, with a temporary return to more frequent feedings during growth spurts. Although breastfeeding will surely start out as the focal point of a new mother's life, with experience and the passage of time, it will evolve into just a part of her life (albeit a supremely satisfying one).

Because formula is digested more slowly than breast milk, bottle-fed infants tend to sleep longer between feedings. Though the newborn will need two or three less feedings per day than her breastfed buddy, parents may be surprised to find that the actual process (and certainly the preparation) takes

quite a while. Bottles, nipples, caps, rings, and all utensils must be scrubbed, boiled, and cooled before being filled with the day's supply of formula. (You can eliminate some of this work by using disposable bottle-bags, or you can eliminate almost all of it by investing in an entirely throw-away bottle system.)

At feeding time, it's necessary first to warm the bottle, then check for proper flow by tilting the bottle and counting the suggested two to three drips per second. (It's probably not a good idea to resolve nipple problems when the baby is screaming to be fed. Just keep a few spares sterilized and assembled for quick switches.) The feeding itself takes between twenty and forty minutes, depending on how quickly the baby summons the two or three burps that will make her most comfortable later on. Then, like her breastfed counterpart, it's time for playing, changing, and putting to sleep—a grand total of at least an hour out of the three or four that pass before it's time to start the process again!

You can streamline both breast and bottle feedings by experimenting to see what setting and position keeps a baby most relaxed and attentive. You can also aid in the emergence of a feeding schedule if you avoid offering food as a pacifier, soothing in other ways when possible. But no matter what the clock says, feed a baby if she's acting truly hungry, for you can rely on her to sense how much and how often to eat (and on the condition of her diapers—six wet and three soiled daily is considered normal—as reassurance).

According to your doctor's recommendations, you'll be adding cereal, then strained fruits, vegetables, and eventually meats to your baby's diet, all starting at around six months. Your baby may resist the thicker consistency at first, or seem to lose most of it in those first clumsy attempts to mash and swallow. But if you keep trying, closing your eyes to the inevitable mess, you'll soon find that spoon-feeding and the introduction of soft finger foods add a new dimension to mealtimes. And just as with breast- and bottle-feeding, you and your baby will both become more proficient with time. Some of the following suggestions may help you along the way:

Breast- and Bottle-feeding an Infant

♥   I used to put one ounce more formula than needed into his bottle. He seemed to take in less air when I ended the feeding before he hit bottom.

♥   Keeping in close contact with people who viewed nursing as a productive, priority activity (and avoiding those who offered sympathy over how tied down I was) helped keep my confidence and spirits up.

♥   To save wear and tear on my back and arm, I used to put a pillow on my lap during a feeding to help hold the baby in place.

♥   *"To relieve the symptoms of engorgement . . . just before nursing, express some milk until the areola softens [and] nurse every two hours, even if you have to wake your baby."*
—Mead-Johnson's *Breastfeeding: The Best Start for Your Baby,* February 1989.

♥   I had a C-section, and rather than have my baby lie across my incision during feedings, I'd lie on my side and feed him from that angle.

♥   I sit sort of sideways, wedged into the V where the back of the couch meets the side. Then I rest my elbow on the side, put the bottle in my other hand and the baby in my lap, and get to work.

♥   As a first-time nurser, I wanted to be sure I got it right. Holding my daughter under my arm and against my side like a football gave me the best view of what she was doing at feedings.

♥   Our baby was the world's most stubborn burper. We made out better by burping him just twice during a feeding—at the middle and at the end—rather than after every two ounces.

♥   *"The average bottle-feeding after the first few weeks of age should last about twenty minutes. If it's lengthier, try making larger holes in the nipple by heating a pin, inserting it in the nipple and leaving it there when running the nipple under cold water."*

—Pediatrician Stuart M. Copperman, M.D.

♥   After a few boilings, no nipple seemed to work as well as it did at first. We learned to cut a fresh "x" in the top, right across any existing slits or holes, for better flow.

♥   I couldn't wait to start taking my baby out. Right from the start I practiced breastfeeding in front of a mirror so that, when the doctor said she was ready to leave the house, I knew I could feed her in public without the world noticing.

♥   *"Hungry bellies have no ears."*

—*The Oxford Dictionary of English Proverbs*, edited by F. P. Wilson, third edition (Oxford University Press, 1970).

♥   I used to recruit someone—anyone—to take one of the daytime feedings while I went for a brisk walk. This way I had a six- or seven-hour break from holding the bottle and actually looked forward to the rest of the day's feedings.

♥   I start nursing on the side that hurts the least. This way, when I switch my baby to the tender side, he's already done with his hardest sucking.

♥   After buying and trying just about every nipple on the market, we settled on classically shaped, clear latex ones. They didn't have that awful rubber taste, they didn't collapse during a feeding, and they seemed to last much longer.

Introducing Solid Food and the Spoon

♥   My baby used to try to "nurse" the spoon at first. I found a very tiny one with a fairly pointed tip that she had an easy time with.

♥   My son had such a big appetite that he would become absolutely hysterical when I started the feeding with a spoonful of cereal; yet after downing eight ounces of formula, he wasn't interested in anything else. We learned to give him half a bottle, the cereal, then the other four ounces.

♥   We started offering my son solids at dinner hour, which seemed to be his least frantic feeding. He was just too impatient in the morning and at noon.

♥   I keep reminding myself that my baby has his own set of taste buds and his own likes and dislikes to go along with them. He doesn't have to prefer chicken to beef, just because it smells better to me; so if he spits something out, I leave it at that.

♥   I gave him his own spoon and bowl to bang with while I fed him with another.

♥   When she rejected spoon after spoon, I started putting a bit of food on my fingertip and letting her suck it off. This way, she had only one new thing at a time to get used to—the spoon itself could come later.

♥ *"Use charts . . . to record what foods are introduced, when each food is started, and your baby's reaction to each food. Review this chart with your physician at baby's next routine visit."*

—Beech-Nut Nutrition Corporation's *Beech-Nut Stages Guide to Infant Feeding,* 1985.

♥ My baby could hold the spoon, but couldn't get it to her mouth until I bought one with a handle that curved sideways. Then the bowl part could reach her mouth without her having to pull her hand all the way up to her face.

♥ My son started solids before he could manage in a high-chair; but in the infant seat, he turned his head so much that food smeared everywhere. Now I line the seat with a bath towel before I sit him down for a "meal."

♥ My son gagged on cereal at first, so I started offering him formula on his spoon. Then, after he was used to sipping it off, I gradually added a few flakes of cereal at a time to thicken it.

♥ My baby always puts her hands in the food dish, but when I try to hold it in my lap I usually wind up spilling it or dripping it on myself. I've just found this great, deep, two-sided dish with a handle that's solved all my problems.

♥ *"I find I get better results with total candor. I put the cards on the table with the Pablum. 'That's right, honey' I say, 'it tastes just like library paste. But remember this—it's full of niacin, thiamin, and riboflavins. Furthermore, you really don't have any taste buds yet, so what's the difference?' "*

—Author and humorist Jean Kerr in *How I Got To Be Perfect* (Doubleday and Co., 1978)

♥ My son tries so hard to spoon-feed himself, but always turns the spoon over just before it gets to his mouth. So I make a special cup of very pasty cereal—thick enough to stay on when the spoon's upside down—and let him practice with it.

♥   I started out offering the baby fruit separately, as a sort of dessert; but when I realized how well it disguised the taste of meat, which she hated, I began mixing everything together.

♥   I allow twice as much time as I think I'll need to feed her, and always feed her *before* her bath.

OLDER BABIES (9 to 15 Months)

Why does food become both a plaything and an enemy?

At the end of baby's first year, parents can expect to encounter new feeding problems. As the solids she's served become more colorful, diverse, and intriguing, the very act of eating simultaneously begins to lose appeal. There are several reasons for this.

By ten to twelve months, she will have a significant drop in both her appetite and growth rate. Though most babies gain a pound to a pound and a half each month at first, you're likely to see a total gain of only three to five pounds during the entire second year. The fact that she's becoming more and more mobile will make time spent in the highchair annoyingly restrictive; in fact, as soon as those already diminished hunger pangs are satisfied, she'll want to be on the move again.

There's really no way to convince a baby to eat; if you resort to songs and games in an effort to sneak in a few extra mouthfuls, she may come to expect such entertainment at every meal. Instead, you can teach her to taste new things and decide for herself when she's done by providing regularly scheduled scaled-down versions of the same meal the rest of the family is having. If you see that she doesn't like something, offering it again two weeks later may bring completely different results. You may be horrified by your baby's nutritional intake on a given day; but research has shown that, if presented with and allowed to choose from a variety of nutritious foods, she'll naturally balance her diet over a week or so.

It's also a good idea to provide a baby with nourishing morning and afternoon snacks each day. Scheduling these snacks between naps and regular meals can pose a challenge, but the effort pays big dividends: between-meal eating can provide up to half her daily calories. When snacks are offered, parents can stop worrying about the meager mouthfuls taken at mealtime.

The older baby may not be particularly interested in eating what's on her plate, but you can count on her to play with it! She'll toss food and utensils on the floor just to hear the sound they make, and your retrieving them will make the game even more fun. She'll be fascinated by the look and feel of whatever she can squash between her fingers and will delight in the smears she creates on the highchair tray. Putting aside housekeeping concerns and allowing a few minutes for this kind of play will give her five senses a healthy workout. It's probably best, however, to remove the food when she shows no further interest in eating. A comment like, "You don't seem to be hungry anymore," gently reinforces the idea that food isn't really a plaything.

The average baby masters the use of a cup and spoon during her second year and, as time passes, will become more businesslike about eating. While you wait for the day when she'll complete a meal without wearing most of it, some of these tips may be helpful:

Eliminating Mealtime Battles With the Older Baby

♥   My son ate best when we served him "fun" food, like vegetables and dip, cheese or meat chunks he could pick up with a spoon, sandwiches cut in shapes, or anything with holes he could poke his finger into.

♥   I serve him less than I think he'll eat and wait till he looks for more. Serving it all at once seems to overwhelm him.

♥   *"Never force a baby to eat or drink anything—they never starve. If baby is not interested in eating, simply take food away and wait for the next meal."*

> —Alvin N. Eden, M.D., father of two and director of pediatrics at Wyckoff Heights Medical Center.

♥   We put her in her highchair in front of the TV. She eats much more when she's distracted by Sesame Street—otherwise, she wants "out" after two bites.

♥   In the afternoon, we put a snack plate, filled with things like string cheese, crackers, and raisins, on a low table where she can help herself as she plays. This way, she's not as cranky by dinnertime; and though she's not as hungry either, at least she's filled up on nourishing things.

♥   We put a gate in the kitchen doorway and then let her roam around the room as she eats. Forcing her to sit only results in hysterics and an uneaten meal.

♥   We played "shark." Each time I turned my head away, he grabbed another piece of food off his plate, supposedly without my seeing. He liked the game, and I liked that he ate dinner.

♥   *"Where there is Hunger, Law is not regarded . . ."*

> —Benjamin Franklin in *Poor Richard's Almanack* (Hallmark Editions, 1967).

♥　We've taken the tray off his highchair so that we can pull the chair to the table at mealtime. He doesn't fuss when he feels like part of the group.

♥　One of us prepares dinner while the other does something really quiet with the baby. If she's calm at mealtime, she'll sit longer.

♥　I serve him the food he likes least—vegetables—first. (He'll eat a few of them when he's very hungry.) Then, after a few minutes, he gets the rest of the meal.

♥　*"If your child craves a snack near mealtime, you can avoid an altercation by giving him part of the meal itself as a snack. Later, at the regular mealtime, he can eat the remainder of his food."*

> —Child psychologist and author Dr. Lawrence Balter in "Eating Behaviors," *Sesame Street Parents' Guide*, November 1989.

♥　I feed her before she has a chance to get really hungry. She may eat lunch at 11:00 and dinner at 4:30, but she eats without a fight.

♥　We look the other way when the food goes all over the place. If we try for neatness, we wind up having a battle; if we leave him alone, he entertains himself as he eats.

♥　If I sat in front of him, he'd push the food aside and try to get out of the chair. If I turned my back and kept busy doing other things, he'd eat much better.

Encouraging the Cup, Self-Feeding, and Variety in an Older Baby's Diet

♥　After a lot of wasted food, we discovered that my daughter would eat crunchy vegetables but not soft ones. Now we give her celery, cucumber, cauliflower, and broccoli—uncooked—and she eats it all.

♥   My son loves bread, but by the fourth bite most of it is stuck to the roof of his mouth. Toasting it lightly and cutting it into small pieces eliminates this problem.

♥   I offer bits of food in different containers. She entertains herself while she eats by filling and dumping them.

♥   *"If you feel guilty about throwing away good food, eat it yourself or feed it to the dog. In a little while, the baby will be feeding it directly to the dog anyway."*

> —Mary Anne Moore in "Turning the Tables on Finicky Eaters," *Parenting* magazine, September 1989.

♥   My son likes colorful food. I put cut-up fruit on his cereal, mix carrots with his potatoes, and even press raisins into his sandwich bread.

♥   I offer a selection at every meal. Even if the only thing she's eating at the moment is ground beef, I serve some of that with a few bites of chicken, some noodles, and a vegetable. Sooner or later, she's tempted to taste something else on her plate.

♥   I noticed that as long as I continued spoon-feeding my baby, he showed little interest in finger foods. When I backed off, he was a lot more motivated to feed himself.

♥   To keep myself from getting crazy over his diet, I first let him pick and choose from a bowl of cut-up foods. Then, once he's lost interest, I supplement whatever he's eaten with some yogurt or cereal.

♥   *"It's a good idea to begin offering babies a sip of milk from the cup each day by the time they're 5 months old."*

> —Dr. Benjamin Spock in *Baby and Child Care* (Pocket Books, 1976).

♥   I used two cups: one with a sipper top for him to hold and suck on, and a different-colored, topless one that I held for him. That way, he got to practice two ways of drinking.

♥ We experimented with at least five different types of sipper cups until we found one with tiny holes that required him to draw very hard in order to get any liquid out. This was not so different from drinking from a bottle, and made the transition easy.

♥ *"Even though a straw makes it easier for a child to drink milk, you may want to encourage a child to drink directly from a glass. Drinking from a glass helps to develop eye-hand coordination."*

   —National Live Stock and Meat Board's *A Good Guide for the First Five Years* (1991).

♥ My daughter gladly traded in her bottle for a juice box— she loved drinking from the tiny straw. Then, when the bottle was truly a thing of the past, I brought out the cup.

♥ We used to practice with cups of water—one-quarter inch of water. This way she could hold the cup by herself, because spills were no big deal.

♥ My baby loves spearing things with his fork. If I serve soft, "stab-able" food, he'll eat almost anything.

5
Speech and Motor Skills

New parents often cannot wait for the day when their baby begins to communicate and move about. Months later, many are still waiting for those first babbles and crawls, while those who've had their wishes granted may already regret them, in light of the fact that baby's speech seems limited to ear-piercing screams and his movements appear to be limited to destructive actions! There are special baby tactics that can help parents encourage their infants' motor skills and speech development, and also provide a safe, enriched environment for the older baby to practice his new-found language and physical achievements. This chapter will explain the techniques that specialists and other parents have used to encourage speech and safe mobility in their own babies. Remember, practice makes perfect!

INFANTS (Newborn to 8 Months)

When do most infants begin verbalizing and getting around?

Infants are completely self-absorbed little things during the first weeks of life, but they start to show their social side just a short time later. As newborns, they tie all their vocalizing in with their physical state as they snuffle and cry to communicate discomfort. But at around four months of age, a baby discovers that he can capture adults' attention with coos and coughs and begins using these sounds purposely to elicit smiles and play.

Just a few weeks later, and to the further delight of his parents, he begins to babble, laugh, and work his mouth in imitation of people speaking to him; and may be clicking his tongue, buzzing, and smacking his lips by the end of month six.

As an infant expands his repertoire of sounds and gestures, parents may find one or two along the way to be more of a problem than an accomplishment. Lip-blowing at mealtime, for example, can have rather unpleasant results; while listening on a hourly basis to a baby determined to reach maximum volume with those high notes takes an even greater toll on the nerves! Curtailing these vocalizations without squelching the baby's enthusiasm can be a delicate matter. . . . After all, his delight in this new-found skill is obvious and certainly more important than any response to a signal for silence.

There are, of course, wide variations in ability among individual babies. Just as one seven-month-old may regularly blurt a crystal-clear "Good boy," the next baby may say nothing recognizable until he's past two. Whichever the case, his vocabulary will expand as his world does; the way you speak and play with him can serve to encourage a baby's babbles and add to the words he understands. It's helpful to keep up a monologue during the course of the day, describing in simple sentences exactly what you and he are doing. Imitating his sounds and answering his noises with words and phrases provides entertainment and promotes the idea of conversation at the same time. In fact, you give his early language skills a boost each time you catch his eye and speak to him directly without competition from other people in the room.

As infants learn to verbalize, their motor skills emerge at the same time. Most of the time, development proceeds from top to toe with the baby achieving head and upper body control long before he's able to crawl or stand. Though motor delays are not unusual, particularly among premature, very large, or extremely verbal infants, the average five-month-old can roll from front to back and may be rocking back and forth in preparation for that first crawl. With prompting and practice, he'll reach, grab, and, if propped, even sit for a few moments by the end of his sixth month.

Whether your infant's motor skills are on, ahead of, or a bit behind schedule, you can encourage his development by providing objects to examine, toys to reach for, and new environments to explore. You can give him the practice he craves by helping him to sit, stand, and sit again during those stages when he can't quite get himself into position. It's also a good idea to allow him the freedom to roam whenever you're close by.

When seven- and eight-month-olds begin to crawl about for the first time, most will try to pull themselves upright on any object in their paths that offers a handhold. Next, most will try climbing, be it up a steep flight of stairs or atop a two-inch-high toy left beside them. By eight months, most are climbing, standing, and falling back down at every opportunity, with their parents left to wonder why they urged their infant along in the first place.

Of course, a baby can't always be on the loose. In fact, restricting movement with the infant seat or playpen may actually have a calming effect when you see that he's become tired or overstimulated. But whatever degree of freedom you allow, the road to baby's mobility will still span as many months as his learning to speak. Here are some tips that may help you both along the way:

Encouraging an Infant's Motor Development

♥   I sit my son in my lap and thumb slowly through an old magazine. He likes patting, wrinkling, and tearing the pictures and tries to turn the pages by himself.

♥   Now that he's standing and trying to take steps, I hold one of his hands and let him use the other to grasp a four-foot piece of dowel that we use as sort of a cane. This keeps him from leaning too far forward.

♥   We make sure she spends a lot of her awake time on her stomach. This forces her to practice head control.

♥   *"To encourage a baby to play with his feet, make a funny foot sock for him."*

> —Dr. Peter L. Mies, psychologist and clinical director of Building Blocks Developmental Preschool.

♥   I hung eight-inch colored ribbons from his mobile. Since they were almost within reach, he'd try to bat and grab at them.

♥   I used to hold back praise until I was sure she recognized her own achievement. (This sometimes meant letting her repeat the action a few times.) This way my praise wouldn't become her motivation.

♥   We blow up a beach ball and let him follow it along the floor. It's light enough that it doesn't take much of a push, and large enough that it can't get stuck anywhere.

♥ Whenever we put her in the stroller, we tie a balloon to the side. She can't quite grab it yet, but she gets lots of practice.

♥ *"I'm very opposed to the use of walkers. They do not aid motor development and in some babies may even delay it. In order to reach full development a child needs to crawl before learning to walk. When parents use walkers they tend to forget that babies need to be down on the floor on their tummies to gain upper body strength. But in the walker, the first thing they learn is to move backwards on their toes."*

—Roni Chastain, R.N., A.C.C.E., visiting nurse for a maternal and child health program and mother of two.

♥ My son was a quiet baby who just wasn't in a hurry to reach those developmental milestones. I learned to let him set the pace, letting his reactions tell me if I was pushing him or offering too much stimulation.

♥ We bought an inexpensive set of colored plastic bowling pins and when she began to crawl, would set them up a few feet down the hall. She'd work really hard to get to them in order to send them flying.

♥ *"Parents who wish to encourage their reluctant walker might rearrange the furniture to create greater distance between the couch, the chair, and the table. . . ."*

—"Kidfile: On Becoming a Toddler," *Parenting* magazine, April 1990.

♥ I keep my eyes peeled for perfect-sized containers to let her play with. Her current favorite is a four-inch screw-top plastic vitamin bottle that I fill with Cheerios.

♥ When he was very tiny, we used to attach bells and tiny rattles to his arms and legs. As he gained control of his limbs, he found different ways to play with these.

♥ We place four pillows side by side on the carpet, then let our daughter crawl, climb, and pull herself over them.

Encouraging Infant Babbles While Discouraging Screeching

♥   We pay close attention to the noise level in our house. His older brother, our dog, appliance noises, and the TV don't do much to encourage baby speech!

♥   Our daughter babbled more when we stopped encouraging her. She wasn't interested in perfecting sounds, just in making them.

♥   When she screeches for amusement, we respond with a gentle and drawn-out "Shhhhhhhhh. . . ." We say nothing else until she stops.

♥   We use a lot of picture books, but I'm very selective. I try to use those with photos, rather than sketches or abstract art, and look for simple pictures of household or familiar neighborhood objects.

♥   We found that she babbled to fill the silence in quiet places but was dumbstruck when in the midst of a lot of noise. Depending on which behavior we wanted to encourage, we knew just the type of places to visit.

♥   I ask a lot of simple questions throughout the course of the day. Although he certainly can't speak yet, the baby often seems to answer with an expression or a gesture.

♥   We discovered by accident that complete silence would bring on the babbles. So for about fifteen minutes a day, I'd put him in his infant seat with several dolls around him and then fade into the background while he "visited" with his friends.

♥   I make an educated guess as to why the baby is screeching and then make a statement that shows I understand, like "Joey feels like being loud today," or "Joey must be ready to get out of the highchair now." A calm voice seems to quiet him down.

♥   *"Make sure you pause sufficiently to give your baby a chance to 'talk.' And rather than always trying to get your baby to react to you, respond to his or her overtures instead."*
—Robert M. McCall, Ph.D., in "Baby 'Talk,' " *Pampers Baby Care, 6–9 Months* (Gruner and Jahr, 1987).

♥   My friend had a very verbal baby just a few months older than mine. Getting them together regularly helped my son's speech development more than any prompting from mommy and daddy.

♥   Whenever the baby decided to practice her shrieking, I'd get the dog to bark at her. It silenced her every time.

♥   When my daughter was about six months, we made her toy phone part of our play routine. I'd babble into it and then pass it to her; soon she was copying my actions and clearly enjoying every minute of it. As an added bonus, I could hand her the toy phone to buy myself a little extra time for a real call.

♥   *"I pitch my voice higher, because small babies are more responsive to higher-pitched voices. Also, when you change your voice to speak to a baby, she knows it's for her."*
—Dr. T. Berry Brazelton in *What Every Baby Knows* (Addison-Wesley, 1987).

♥   If her screams reached the ear-splitting level, everyone around her would lower their voices to a whisper and pretend to have a very animated conversation. She'd quiet down just to hear what was going on.

♥   My son did most of his babbling when he was alone. To encourage him, I used to put him down for the night when he was still in a good mood and let him talk himself to sleep. He'd get as much as twenty minutes of "practice" every day.

OLDER BABIES (9 to 15 Months)

What sort of speech and motor skills are typical of nine- to fifteen-month-olds?

Though a few babies may speak their first word by ten months, most at this age are more likely to be busy at a sort of conversational gibberish. There's no evidence that an early talker is a brighter child—these expressive babbles simply serve as reassurance that his vocal equipment will work when the baby is ready to speak. In the meantime, the fact that he mimics the same gestures, inflections, and sounds that he sees and hears around him reveals how much he absorbs just by listening.

You can see by his holding out a foot when he hears "shoe" or by his glance toward the refrigerator at the mention of "juice" that a baby's understanding of dozens of words precedes the use of even one or two. And even when he does finally blurt out "lie" for light or "cckk" for cookie, you may be disappointed to find that these early words disappear from his vocabulary a little later on. Babies must coordinate many signals before words can begin to flow, and most babies don't have the process ironed out until around fifteen months of age.

Throughout much of the second year, a baby's speaking vocabulary lags far behind what he'd like to say. You can expect him to become extremely frustrated when he can't make himself understood; but a little guesswork and a lot of patience can often keep screaming and foot-stomping from becoming habit. As with infants, it's a good idea to offer a simple but descriptive narration of what's happening, like "Michael is walking in the snow." It's also helpful to elaborate on words or gestures the baby uses, as in "Baw!"/"Michael sees a ball." And this same technique can be used to demonstrate pronunciation without actually correcting your baby: "Muk!"/"Does Michael want some milk?"

Older babies work just as hard at achieving mobility and an upright stance as they do at forming that first word, though not always at the same time. As he enters and continues through his second year, a baby may appear to take turns practicing motor and verbal skills, almost as though each requires his complete and undivided attention. So in many cases, the active and curious baby will begin to talk much later than his placid counterpart, who is often more looker-listener than mover. Parents can help by following the baby's lead: if he's into climbing this week, work with him on the stairs rather than drag out the picture books.

The fact that nearly 25 percent of babies can take a few steps at ten months, while another 10 percent are still not walking by fifteen months, is proof that each develops new skills as he's ready to do so. Most prewalking ten-month-olds are able to stand with little support. They can sit down from a standing position and pull themselves upright again, while sharpening their climbing skills every chance they get. As they struggle toward complete mobility, prewalkers may become frustrated by their own limitations. They will demand to be carried and entertained more than usual, until their motor skills catch up with their ambition to be completely mobile.

Just five months later, nearly all babies have abandoned crawling for walking. They're not yet able to alter the length of each step, but most can increase the number of steps in order to get where they're going in a hurry. As a walker, a baby may seem suddenly happier; traveling by foot enables him to satisfy his curiosity and keep himself a lot busier than before.

This exciting mobility brings with it a few problems, not the least of which are frequent tumbles resulting from mis-

judged distances or attempts to pick up speed. You can dis-
courage the almost-walker's tendency to tempt fate by leaning
forward if you hold him by one hand instead of by his upraised
arms.

The most important thing you can do for your traveling
baby is to provide him with a safe environment. Examining
each room from his vantage point, on hands and knees if
necessary, can turn up an unforeseen hazard or two. It's also
wise to invest in a household safety kit containing corner
pads, cabinet locks, outlet plugs, doorknob covers, and the
like.

No matter how rigid your safety standards, a baby who is
not in the crib or the playpen is never truly safe. Stay with
him when he's on the loose. The following list offers some
helpful suggestions for building his skills while keeping him
out of harm's way:

Safeguarding the Newly Mobile Baby

♥   I ran a dry sponge over all of our wood floors, looking for
splinters and nail heads. If the sponge snagged, so would the
baby's clothing, and I knew a repair was needed.

♥   I found a concise, easy-to-read first-aid chart, pho-
tocopied it, and tacked copies in every room of the house.
Help was right at hand if we needed it.

♥   I gave away all my houseplants and would buy for out-
doors only those plants that my gardening book assured me
were safe.

♥   *"Parents should let their young children decide for themselves how much they are going to attempt, find their own
supports, and get out of difficult situations by themselves.
Parents should not keep saying, 'Watch out,' but instead
should let the child herself become watchful, attentive to her
own safety and aware of the risks she is taking."*

—Author and kinesiotherapist Dr. Janine Levy in *You and Your Toddler:
Sharing the Developing Years* (Random House, 1975).

♥   My daughter is slight and wiry. Seat belt and all, she could still wriggle her way to a standing position in the highchair. I began running a second belt across her chest, under her arms, and around the back of the chair. Now, at least, I feel safe turning my back for a moment.

♥   The day I found my son proudly perched on the sill was the day I began opening my windows from the top. If a baby's agile enough to climb into the window, no screen is going to hold him in!

♥   My baby is fascinated by the kitchen garbage can and its contents. We now keep a second, smaller one just for him, into which we toss enough empty boxes and containers to keep him out of our dinner scraps.

♥   We collect our guests' coats, keys, and handbags and lock them in our bedroom. Our house may be babyproofed, but our company's possessions present new temptation.

♥   *"Use the gate as little as possible, and try to resolve the situation by helping the child learn to negotiate the stairs by himself, both up and down, as soon as he is physically able to do so. A useful procedure is to place a gate at the third or fourth step, rather than at the bottom."*

—Author and noted psychologist Burton L. White, Ph.D., in *The First Three Years of Life* (Prentice-Hall, 1975).

♥   I packed away all my tablecloths the day my baby tried to pull himself up on a dangling corner and instead pulled a whole place setting down around him.

♥   We toss towels over the tops of the doors to her bedroom and playroom. This eliminates the possibility of her closing herself in or pinching her fingers.

♥   *"To foil a little phone operator, try putting a wide rubber band over the contact points. This way, you won't be out of commission when the phone is knocked off the hook, and the child won't be able to dial any long-distance numbers."*
   —Jan Hart Sousa in "A Child-Proof Home," *Parents Baby Care, 9–12 Months*
   (Gruner and Jahr USA Publishing, 1987).

♥   For several weeks when our daughter was first walking, we'd wrap a Velcro-fastened cervical collar around her head like a crown. She still fell a lot, but the tumbles were painless.

♥   I built a gate by the steps leading from our deck, making it like a giant playpen. This gave my son some freedom out-doors and gave us some peace of mind.

♥   Our baby insisted on being underfoot when we worked in the kitchen. We bought covers for the two front stove burners to remind us to do our cooking on the rear burners only.

Strengthening the Older Baby's Listening Skills and Vocabulary

♥   When my first daughter was born, most of our friends were still childless. Spending time around adults who spoke to her in the same tone of voice they used for each other, rather than in baby talk, helped her use more adult-like speech.

♥   My daughter is extremely active. Calling to her over my shoulder or from another room never gets her attention; since I don't want her to get in the habit of tuning me out, I force myself not to speak at all unless we're actually face to face.

♥ Whenever we shop, we play a game. When I pick an item from the shelf or rack, I hold it up and say its name. If my son attempts to name it, he gets to toss the item into the cart—his favorite job.

♥ *"I use picture cards from a lotto game. [The original lotto game contained cards showing pictures, letters, and numbers.] My son likes to handle them and throw them around; when a picture he can recognize lands near us, I point to it and name the object."*

—Speech/language pathologist Elissa Chekow Dembner, M.A., C.C.C.-S.P.

♥ My daughter had a long-playing music box. I'd wind it up, hide it somewhere and have her follow the sounds to its hiding place.

♥ Several times a day, I stop what we're doing and ask him what he hears. After a bit of practice listening, he now points to the sky if there's a plane, in addition to trying to imitate the sound of things like the dishwasher and the fire siren.

♥ *"Be swift to hear; and let thy life be sincere; and with patience give answer."*

—Burton Stevenson, Ed., *The Home Book of Bible Quotations,* Ecclesiasticus v, 11 (Harper and Brothers, 1949).

♥ I used to cut out pictures of things she'd recognize, mount them on six-by-six-inch paper, and slide them into plastic sandwich bags. When the bags were sewn together, we'd have a waterproof, fairly sturdy homemade "book."

♥ My daughter hides her eyes while I hide a raisin somewhere nearby. I tell her where it can be found, but she has to first identify the object—book, doll, shoe, toy, table, etc.—that I've used as a hiding place.

♥ We played games with empty toilet paper rolls and plastic containers, which he'd either toot into or hold over his ears in order to hear the roar.

♥   I made a tape of common noises like a car horn, a dog barking, or a ringing phone and cut out pictures of these same objects. I'd play the tape while we matched the pictures with the noises.

♥   *"I'd draw a circle for a face and ask, 'What does this person need?' If she said 'nose,' I'd draw in a nose; if she said 'eye,' I'd draw in one eye, and so on until the face was complete. As time went on, the faces became more elaborate."*

—Speech pathology major Alyce Farina, mother of two.

♥   We borrowed lots of simple storybook-and-cassette sets from the library. He liked listening to someone else's voice reading the same two- or three-word sentences over and over.

♥   I do a lot with rhythm instruments. Sometimes we try to copy each other's rhythms, sometimes we try to match the instrument with the sound, and sometimes we just play.

♥   We use a lot of requests, like "Go get your shoes," "Give the doll a stroller ride," or "Put your bottle in the sink," and praise her to the skies when she follows through.

6

Relationships With Other Children

The presence of a tiny playmate or an older sibling can add a special dimension to the life of a baby, but along with the beginnings of social behavior come complications. Smiling and babbling while interacting with another child can give way to fussing and conflicts, particularly when the children are mismatched in size or temperament. Struggles between siblings are equally common. To cope with dividing time between an older sibling and an infant, or with aggression, disinterest, or timidity among baby and her siblings and friends, parents will need certain baby tactics. This chapter offers the solutions of other parents and babycare experts for encouraging the positive side of their own babies' early relationships. Man the battle stations!

INFANTS (Newborn to 8 Months)

How is infant care different when a sibling is present?

Most parents cheerfully lose themselves in the joy, wonder, and round-the-clock care of their first baby, but things are often a bit different the second or third time around. When older brothers and sisters are present (and particularly if they're preschoolers), you may sense that every feeding, cuddling, and diaper-changing session with the new competition is being observed with suspicion. In return, you'll find yourself watching just as carefully each time your older child ventures toward her new sibling, wondering all the while whether you should suppress the impulsive hugs and kisses you bestowed so freely when they themselves were babies!

Confusion and disturbance about a new sibling on the part of big brother or sister is certainly understandable. Chances are they didn't ask for this new baby, so you can't really expect them to relinquish their king-of-the-hill role with a smile! To small children, every bit of care you give the new baby is apt to seem like time stolen from them; older children may understand the demands of infancy but know exactly who's to blame each time the family must skip an activity or leave a gathering early.

"At least we don't have to walk him."

Things don't necessarily improve over the next few months, for as baby begins to smile, coo, and move about, she may receive even more attention than when she was newborn. And while she gathers praise for each new milestone, the older child must lose access to some favorite toys for the sake of baby's safety and is told to play with the others behind closed doors in order to keep them intact!

There will be many occasions when the big sister or brother chooses to act as "teacher," gaining both confidence and enjoyment from time spent with the baby. But eventually, either the baby will have had enough of such controlling behavior or the older child will have bored of the activity. At this point, you'll have to step in to avoid trouble.

Most parents quickly discover that they can tend to their infant's physical needs and give attention to big brother or sister at the same time. You can buy some much-needed time by anticipating your older child's snack or entertainment needs before settling down to baby's feeding or bathtime. Occasionally stepping in to entertain the baby when her tiny presence becomes intrusive shows that you also respect the older child's right to play undisturbed. When big sister or brother's face clouds over at the sight of you with the baby, it helps to show empathy by putting their negative feelings into words. You can also give their egos an occasional boost by commiserating over the baby's helplessness.

Catering to an older child's feelings of displacement while still getting across the point that the new baby is a normal and permanent family member can be a very difficult job. Here are some suggestions that may help:

Dividing Your Time Between Infant and Sibling

♥   We tried to avoid too much parental "pairing off," as in dad feeding the baby while mom took big brother to the park. Though that sort of thing made life easy in the short run, it did nothing at all to help our older child deal with his jealousy.

♥   I set a kitchen timer for the thirty or so minutes I'll need for the baby's feeding or bath. My older girl amuses herself while she waits for the bell that signals *our* playtime and hasn't caught on that, when I'm running behind schedule, I sometimes give the dial an extra little twist.

♥   We staged a once-a-week "Grandma Day," on which my mother would take my daughter to lunch, to the park, or to the library. These few hours were a change of pace for my somewhat house-bound daughter and much appreciated by the baby and me.

♥   I used to prop the baby in the infant seat and set up an activity with my older child right in his line of vision. Our play would entertain the baby as well.

♥   After the children are in bed for the night, I set up three or four intriguing-looking activities in the playroom. I settle big sister in there after the next day's breakfast, giving me a half hour or more alone with baby.

♥   We went out for a stroll nearly every morning when the baby was tiny. She'd fall asleep in the Snugli, and my son and I could hold hands, walk, and talk just like in the old days.

♥   I asked a neighborhood preteen, whom he loves dearly, to play with my older son for an hour every day after school. Those five hours of time I had with the baby were well worth the fifteen dollars a week.

♥   *"Find a balance that allows them time for being a part of each other's lives and time for being apart from one another, experiencing the benefits of both."*

—Psychotherapist and mother Mara Sandler.

♥   I made use of local activities like story time and craft class for the older one and would use the hour that she was busy to play somewhere in or near the building with the little one.

♥ I use nursing the baby as the signal for a sit-down activity with the older child. The baby's nursing seems almost incidental to the puzzles we do or the picture we're coloring.

♥ *"If you're [with] your firstborn and the baby wakes up . . . you somehow need to convey the fact that finishing that activity is very important to you, but that he has to wait for a few minutes."*

—Denise Schipani in "The New Kid in Town," *Child,* April 1990.

♥ *"The older child can be dubbed 'babysitter' when you're close by. . . . Finding that they have the ability to entertain baby is ego-boosting to senior sisters and brothers."*

—Author and professional medical writer Arlene Eisenberg, et al. in "When Firstborn Meets Newborn," *Working Mother,* June 1989.

♥ As a special treat when I need a few minutes, I allow my older son to play in the baby's room. There may be only rattles and infant toys in there, but because they're not what he's used to, he finds them fascinating.

♥ I put together a basket of odds and ends like paper scraps and glue, novelty pens and markers, stickers, magazines, ribbons, finger puppets, beads and string. By changing the contents frequently, I could rely on the basket to entertain our oldest when the baby was fussy.

♥ We had a box of homemade hats, badges and other "accessories" which enabled him to play chef, policeman, fireman, doctor, or whatever he was into that day. The rule was that his pretend box came out only once a day and at my sayso; the fact that his use of it was limited made it all the more absorbing.

Coping With Aggressive or Disinterested Siblings

♥ We put a gate in the doorway of the older one's room. He could play undisturbed but still interact with his audience, the baby.

♥   He likes to be reminded that everything done for the baby was once done for him, too. As we tend to the baby, we relate story after story about his own infancy, each one ending with a comment on how very grown-up he is now.

♥   I sometimes used to let my older boy play in the baby's playpen. He seemed to get satisfaction out of invading his brother's space, for a change.

♥   *"In trying to keep older children from doing permanent physical damage to their juniors, it is probably not advisable to adopt the tit-for-tat type of punishment ('If you pull Billy's hair again, I'm going to pull your hair!'). . . . When it comes right down to it, you can't really punch that kid straight in the eye or spit in his milk."*

> —Jean Kerr in *How I Got To Be Perfect* (Doubleday and Co., 1978).

♥   We suspected that our older boy's disinterest in the baby was an act. To draw him out, we made a point of spending time around other families with new babies, letting him see the kinds of interactions that were possible.

♥   I started teaching my older boy gentle behavior as soon as we learned his brother was on the way. We studied other people's babies, petted animals, and practiced his new gentleness on dolls. It was old hat by the time the baby was born.

♥   *"Children's books can help older siblings contend with their feelings and perhaps see the new arrangement in a more favorable light."*

> —Writer Leonard S. Marcus in "Sibling Library," *Parenting* magazine, June/July 1989.

♥   We found that it helped to balance the concessions made necessary by her new brother's presence with some privileges. When we brought the baby home, we extended our daughter's bedtime and allowed her a few new rights like playing outside alone and signing up for gymnastics.

♥ I refer frequently to my older girl's own first-year photo album. Seeing herself in the same baby tub and gnawing on some of the same toys as the baby does seems to offset some of her jealousy.

♥ We allow him to "overhear" us talking to the baby about how lucky she is to have a big brother. Somehow, the words have more weight when they're spoken to someone else—we can count on these episodes to bring on some sort of loving brotherly gesture.

♥ My son pretty much ignored the baby until one day when I left them alone for a moment. When I returned to find him stroking her face and speaking softly to her, I realized that I had to step back more often and let them interact.

♥ *"When the third child came along, the oldest complained, 'Mommy, you're always feeding that baby!' I realized I was nursing the baby when he left for school and when he came home, so I changed the baby's schedule. . . ."*

—Psychologist Patricia Nilson, Ph.D., mother of three.

♥ Our son's aggression began when the baby started crawling and getting into his toys. Since they were hardly ready to learn cooperation, I soon stopped trying to police their play. Instead, I concentrated on having them play completely apart from one another.

♥ We allow the expression of anger, but insist that she "make up" with the baby afterwards by apologizing, hugging, or whatever's necessary.

♥ Both my husband and I come from large families. When our older child seems troubled about the baby, we draw a story from our own childhoods that parallels whatever he's going through. Talking about how we felt helps him to open up.

OLDER BABIES (9 to 15 Months)

What type of socialization can you really expect from a baby?

As a rule, children don't begin to interact as real playmates until the age of three. But giving even an infant access to other children can provide her, a bit at a time, with the building blocks of social behavior.

Many babies become rather clingy at seven months or so; then, as eight-month-olds, they experience some degree of stranger anxiety. Their separation fears often work in tandem with this uneasy fascination with strangers, resulting in a baby who will fix a solemn and unwavering gaze on people both big and small—as long as she's safely ensconced in mom or dad's arms and those unfamiliar faces keep their distance. Encouraging her as she peeks over your shoulder and warms up to strangers at her own speed will help her feel secure while she satisfies any curiosity about what they may be doing.

The very first seeds of social behavior begin to sprout a month or so later. As nine-month-olds, babies are able to recognize the difference between children and grownups, and begin to find each other pretty fascinating. They'll smile and babble when seated together, sometimes reaching out a tentative hand to touch each other's face or hair. At this age, some babies may be quite aggressive, while their more timid pals, easily frightened by commotion, are quick to protest when the other gets too close. Then it's up to the adults to intervene, either by demonstrating the desired gentle behavior or by providing some merciful distraction.

At one year of age, even the outgoing baby still views other children as mere physical beings. She's likely to push and grab in their presence, for she doesn't understand (or care) how her behavior affects others. She's also impulsive, acting on whatever notion happens to strike. But she can now begin to communicate with pals by imitating the pace and volume of their play while she tries to duplicate their actions. If she doesn't feel ready for a new social situation, you may well find her glued to either your lap or your leg, but a bit of "protection" from an attentive parent usually sets her back on course in no time.

By fifteen months, most babies delight in watching and playing alongside one another. It's far too early for them to share or take turns, so there's no sense in your requesting good manners when trouble strikes. If you demonstrate the behavior you expect and remove her from the area if she cannot follow through, a baby can learn what's acceptable by observation. You can help diffuse too-physical situations by stepping in immediately when one playmate starts to become aggressive, offering a distracting substitute activity.

It's important to make play dates a time of enjoyment for both you and your baby by encouraging and praising these first fumbling steps toward appropriate social behavior. The following tactics may help you:

Encouraging a Socially Reluctant Older Baby

♥ With our very timid baby, we concentrated on only the simplest social skills—those which could be practiced in almost any setting: hi, bye, please, and thank you. Playgroups and other kids could come later.

♥ I found that my son was much less threatened by children who were younger (and so, less physical and verbal) than he was. For a long time, this was our main criterion when inviting someone over.

♥ We had success with a baby-gym program. In a room so large that noise just seemed to get lost, I could stay right by my son's side while the music and play equipment distracted him from the presence of fifteen others like him.

♥ I rent old Romper Room videos and try to tape any kids' programs that show groups of small children. I show these while she's playing nearby so that she'll get used to "company"—even if it's two-dimensional.

♥   *"Having warm, supportive, and encouraging parents to which the child feels deeply, securely, and affectionately attached seems to be basic to the development of social competence."*

> —Lilian G. Katz, Ph.D., early-childhood education professor, in "Making Friends," *Parents*, November 1987.

♥   My friend and I use side-by-side playpens. Our babies can interact if they want, but have their own space, too.

♥   My son became very agitated in groups. For months, we simply avoided them, substituting a weekly date with just one neighborhood mom and baby with whom he was very familiar.

♥   Despite my daughter's wails, we continued to go to playgroup. At first, we stayed just long enough to say hello, then started watching the others for longer and longer stretches until the place and people no longer frightened her.

♥   *"Help your child practice meeting people through role play between the child and dolls or puppets."*

> —Clinical psychologist Joan Shapiro, Ph.D., in "She's Just Shy," American Baby's *Healthy Kids: Birth–3*, Spring/Summer 1990.

♥ My baby did much better in familiar surroundings than in someone else's house, so I convinced my mothers' group to let me host our get-togethers for a few months.

♥ We made a lot of unnecessary trips to toy and children's clothing stores just to watch other babies. My son felt comfortable, probably because most of the little people were confined to strollers, so I'd cruise the aisles, pointing out and commenting on what each one was doing. A dozen or so kids later, we'd call it a morning.

♥ *"Don't hover. Researchers notice that the presence of an intrusive adult inhibits interaction and conversation. Toddlers play in more sophisticated ways when adults are not in control."*
—Writer Ruth Mason, mother of two, in "First Friends," *Parents*, October 1990.

♥ We limited get-togethers to just forty-five minutes and each brought an unusual toy from home. By the time the babies finished trying everything out and were starting to get in each other's way, it was time to leave.

♥ I'd ask a friend to leave her baby with me for an hour or so. This eliminated the distraction of adult conversation and left me free to "lead" side-by-side activities like dancing and water play.

♥ My neighbor's baby happened to be on a similar schedule to mine, so twice a week we'd serve them lunch together. They'd look suspicious when we first sat them side by side, but eating kept them busy enough not to object too strongly.

Taming the Aggressive Older Baby

♥ Before another child comes over, I hide away whatever toys my baby's most enchanted with at the time. This doesn't eliminate all the screaming, but if a toy has been in her hand all morning, she's certainly more likely to become physical about sharing or not sharing it.

♥   For a while, I'd put out only those playthings that I could provide two of. This sometimes meant playing with empty boxes, bowls, and spoons; but the babies didn't mind and their frustration was kept to a minimum.

♥   I used to bring in an equally aggressive playmate. We spent a lot of time separating the babies, but each got a taste of what it was like on the receiving end of all that energy, and neither became the victim.

♥   *"Leave off while the play is good."*
        —*The Oxford Dictionary of English Proverbs*, edited by F. P. Wilson, third
          edition (Oxford University Press, 1970).

♥   I find that adding a third baby to the playtime picture tends to dilute some of my daughter's overly physical behavior. It makes it much harder for her to zero in on a victim.

♥   When my baby starts getting wild at playgroup, I say, "You cannot play because you're not being gentle today." Then we leave without another word. He'll learn self-control eventually, but I don't want aggression to become a habit in the meantime.

♥   We try to spend time around some of the three- and four-year-olds in the neighborhood. They interact, they share, and they make good social models for my baby.

♥   My son seems to reserve his out-of-control behavior for home. In public, he's usually pretty agreeable. Needless to say, I encourage invitations to play rather than extend them myself.

♥   *"You should remove him from the room to cool down. After he is calm, you should empathize with him. . . . Tell him that you understand his feelings and that you want to help him find a way to continue to play with his friend."*
        —Sandra Wolkoff, C.S.W., in Neala Schwartzberg, Ph.D., "Teaching Your Child
          How to Fight the Good Fight," *Child*, January/February 1990.

♥   When I see signs of aggression, I interrupt her play with some kind of parent-led activity. Almost anything works, because it takes the focus off the other child and puts it on me instead.

♥   Since he's way too young to understand rules, we prefer that our child play alone. Sure, there's still some degree of frustration when things don't go right, but we'd rather see him bash a toy than bash another baby.

♥   *"An effective way for parents to diffuse power struggles is to find an acceptable way for children to practice a new skill. Children who insist on throwing, for example, may be given a set of beanbags. . . ."*

> —Marilyn Segal, Ph.D., and Don Adcock, Ph.D., in *Your Child at Play* (Newmarket Press, 1985.)

♥   I tried to coach him to turn his aggressive energy into noise. When the grabbing and screaming would start, I'd hand him a saucepan and a wooden spoon and would encourage him to bang away.

♥   Even though it will be a while before he understands, we always talk to our son about caring, consideration, and other people's feelings. You'd be surprised at how many opportunities there are to point out kindnesses!

♥   It always seemed to us that children from volatile households were just as loud and heavy-handed when they were on their own. We tried to set a different example by treating our children gently and respectfully.

7
Setting Limits

All babies need some sort of structure and order in their lives, if only to avoid the dangers to which their natural curiosity and self-centeredness can lead them! There are particular baby tactics that have proven useful to parents and child-rearing authorities who needed to modify their babies' behavior. This chapter presents their suggestions on establishing limits in an infant's world, and on circumventing willfulness in or effectively disciplining the older baby. Remember, patience is a virtue!

INFANTS (Newborn to 8 Months)

Does an infant really need discipline?

To many parents, the word "discipline" connotes punishment for deliberate misbehavior. This is not really the case. The word itself stems from "disciple," or "one who receives instruction from another" (*Webster's Dictionary for Everyday Use*, Ottenheimer Publishers, 1981). Rather than inflicting some sort of physical or psychological penalty, true discipline is more a matter of gently shaping behavior—particularly in infancy!

A baby as young as three or four months can understand the relationship between cause and effect, and begins to put it to use in a primitive fashion to bring a parent to his side. (The habit of off-schedule night waking is a perfect example.) And, though he can't control most of the actions that consistently bring him a smile or a frown, your baby does understand the difference between the two.

Just a short time later, the ability to comprehend approval begins to emerge. By recognizing with smiles and praise the many accomplishments that punctuate an infant's first months, parents create the first stirrings of baby's desire to achieve. It's a good idea to introduce a bit of frustration at the same time by gently coaxing him into a feeding schedule or occasionally offering a diverting toy in place of the pacifier or mommy's arms. By five months, a baby will usually accept these early exercises in self-discipline; by teaching him to cope with limits gradually rather than imposing them all at once when the need arises, you're actually doing him a favor!

It's important for infants to learn (but often difficult to convey) exactly what behavior is unacceptable in your household, whether it be head-banging, food-spitting, or pulling up on the fireplace screen. Parents unknowingly present such limits each time they offer a substitute for an undesirable activity or move to protect their infant from pain and danger. Though a baby of this age can't yet understand the word "no," he can learn limits from the context the "no" is used in and from your firmness and consistency in steering him away from the objectionable.

Keep your infant's natural immaturity in mind when he heads in the wrong direction. He doesn't intend to thwart you each time he bashes a toy against the coffee table; he's just showing off a new accomplishment! There will be less stress for all concerned if you can provide an environment in which he can explore freely and safely.

An infant only has the capacity for "needs," not "wants." By asserting these needs, he's doing only what comes naturally to him. You can help by being vigilant and firm while you wait for that far-off day when he'll be able to exercise self-control. Here are some tips that may help in the meantime:

Avoiding Incidences of Undesirable Behavior in Infants

♥ On days that I must tamper with my baby's sleep schedule, he really makes us pay! To encourage his good-natured side instead, I do whatever I can to ensure that he gets proper naps.

♥ No matter how much I may have needed those few minutes during which he was engrossed in knocking stacks of diapers off the changing-table shelf, I made sure my responses were consistent. If it wasn't allowed on day one, it was never allowed.

♥   She may be only six months old, but we take pains to treat our baby politely and with respect. It's our hope that, by making her feel exceptionally good about herself, she'll always respond in kind to others.

♥   *"Avoid trying to control situations that cannot be controlled. . . . [For example,] nothing can force the child to sleep. Insisting that they must . . . invites an unnecessary battle."*

> —Alvin Rosenfeld, M.D., and Dorothy Levine, M.D., in "Parenting Q & A," *American Baby*, June 1990.

♥   Now that my son is crawling, I make it a point to gate off the kitchen and living room and keep all doors except his own closed. When his travel is limited to the nursery and hallway, so is the trouble he can get into.

♥   Ours is a busy house, and we knew we wouldn't be able to carry our new baby around for great lengths of time. We made use of the infant seat from the day she came home, packing her in with blankets and keeping her close by for plenty of stroking and patting. Being "down" soon felt as natural to her as being held.

♥   *"If after the first few months your baby's schedule is running you ragged and she's crying and fussing for what seems like no good reason, chances are your well-intentioned accommodation to her demands has run amok. Parents at this point should try to create a workable routine—and stick to it."*

> —Jean Callahan in "Who's Running the Show?" *Parenting* magazine, June/July 1990.

♥   Experts may call for consistency, but I prefer to be flexible in handling my baby. Some days she's just more needy than other days; when this happens, I ignore the baby-care books and let her spend as many hours in my arms as she needs to.

♥ Whether they personally agree or not, we make sure that every adult involved in her care understands our specific behavioral goals and uses the discipline methods we've decided upon.

♥ When we're away from home, I keep him in his stroller constantly. This eliminates the need for me to play policewoman while visiting and seems to keep him happier than, say, being plopped on a strange-looking rug among toys he's never seen before.

♥ From the very beginning, I used a gentle back-scratching to soothe my daughter into a good mood. Things always went smoothly when she was relaxed and contented.

♥ *"Discipline [is] . . . at this time a matter of thinking largely in terms of what [your child] is able to do—both physically able and emotionally able—and then seeing to it that your demands fall within the limits of these abilities."*
—Louise Bates Ames, et al. in *Your One Year Old* (Delacorte Press, 1982).

♥ I look for target times for, shall we say, "unpleasant" behavior in my baby. Wherever and whenever there seems to be a pattern, I just change his routine.

♥ As an infant, my son had the most trouble when my attention was directed elsewhere. Praying that this was a temporary condition, I put myself at his complete disposal by passing major chores to my husband and by rising an hour before the baby in order to get a jump on the day.

♥ Before each new undertaking, I look ahead and decide which habits I don't want to deal with down the line—blanket-toting at the park or whining for snacks in the store, for example. I then try to meet all my baby's needs before leaving home and make each venture short enough not to arouse them again.

Shaping Infant Behavior

♥   We watch our tone of voice when correcting her. Reacting to negative behavior without emotion makes it seem like less of a game.

♥   I see a lot more "testing" done by babies from homes where only one parent acts as disciplinarian. Even though my husband and I have different tolerance levels and though one of us is much more available, we make a strong effort to share this job.

♥   *" 'Don't'—slap—'Stop it'—whack—'Don't.' Throughout this strange and painful ritual, the child smiles benignly or cries noisily, utterly incapable of understanding what's going on. [It's] . . . so much easier just to lift temptation out of reach."*
          —Christopher Green, M.D., in *Dr. Green's Baby Book* (Fawcett Columbine, 1988).

♥   For now, we avoid negative words. We get the same good results with a frown and headshake as we move the baby away from the offending object.

♥   When I had to take something away from her, I acted really excited about whatever I substituted, saying something like "Wow! Look what I have for you! A _____!" This made it more like a gift than a trade-off.

♥   We make sure to treat accidents differently than mis-behaviors, which seem intentional. We want her to realize that there are consequences to her actions.

♥   We believe in "killing with kindness"—smiles, praise, applause, and hugs for behavior we want to encourage.

♥   *"I used to let them get to the point of almost-disaster, then shout 'No!' That way they knew exactly what was wrong and why it might be dangerous or forbidden."*
          —Freelance children's writer Carole Forman, mother of three.

♥   I saved my fierce reactions for really dangerous things, like touching the stove or sticking an arm through a railing. The rest of the time, I just moved him away.

♥   Each time I corrected my son, I repeated verbatim whatever simple rule applied to the situation. I think the monotony eventually discouraged him from trying again.

♥   We try to be flexible, because no discipline tactic works *all* the time. As long as we're consistent about the behaviors we won't allow, any number of "consequences" can be used to get the message across.

♥   There's too much potential for danger and frustration when the baby is let loose among her brother's toys. To encourage play that's less traumatic, I insist that they play separately unless I'm running a special activity that they can both handle.

♥   If the baby is getting into repeated trouble, it's usually because he's overdoing the physical activity. By putting him in the highchair with something he's never seen before, like an old deck of cards or some refrigerator magnets, I calm him down.

♥   When we have a mishap, I try to step back, examine the situation clinically, and pinpoint why it happened. Did I expect too much? Was she too stimulated? This helps prevent a recurrence.

OLDER BABIES (9 to 15 Months)

Why do older babies sometimes become demanding and destructive?

Just as in infancy, the older baby is incapable of willful disobedience. It's unfair to judge his responses to various situations in terms of right versus wrong, for they're more a function of his physical and emotional immaturity. As a crawling, exploring baby, he's apt to get into almost constant trouble; and it's natural for him to be frustrated by the many "don'ts" that suddenly appear in his life.

Babies pass through different stages in their struggle to absorb the limits set at home. When they begin to get around, they'll reach out a hand to touch something forbidden and, ignoring verbal admonishments, keep it there until they're physically removed from temptation. A month or so later, they'll reach for the same object, but turn to look at their parent in anticipation of the word "no." This usually coincides with the first displays of guilt following either a wrongdoing or a scolding.

As he enters his second year, a baby usually begins to respond to directions, having learned to like the parental approval he receives after following through. He will still touch a forbidden object, but will correct himself with either a "no" or an "uh-uh" and then wait patiently for praise. (Only much later, as he approaches three years of age, will he achieve the self-control necessary to approach the object, think "no," and *not* touch it.)

There are certain age-related behaviors that are almost unavoidable in the older baby. Most pass through such phases as aimless screeching, toy throwing, and the knocking down of any unsecured tabletop item. In most cases, this behavior lasts only a few months; and, if not preventable, can be avoided or worked around for the duration. As always, gentle but steadfast discipline techniques are more effective than punishment. Most older babies will learn to accept restrictions if they're repeated many times, particularly if their self-esteem is bolstered by recognition of any appropriate behavior.

A baby can only learn self-discipline with his parents' help. As he faces constraints for the first time, he may be confused and frustrated by his loss of control; and when this happens, he needs their calm reassurance more than commiseration or a "he'll-get-used-to-it" attitude. With patience and an occasional air of compromise (for it's unrealistic to expect him to conform at every turn), you can guide your baby's behavior without a constant battle of wills. These ideas may help you:

Averting Willfulness in the Older Baby

♥ I don't look for obedience and consideration from my daughter. This way, I'm pleasantly surprised when she does cooperate, but not frustrated by her normal behavior.

♥ I find that being super-organized gives me the opportunity to anticipate almost every clash. Most can be avoided by planning ahead; for the others, I always have "plan B" ready as a diversion.

♥ We don't compare our son to other babies. Gazing in envy at the docile little charmer down the street only seems to magnify our own son's stubborn streak; we try instead to focus our energy on dealing with his more difficult but perfectly normal temperament.

♥ *"Give a child till he craves, and a dog while his tail doth wave, and you'll have a fair dog, but a foul knave."*

> —*The Oxford Dictionary of English Proverbs*, edited by F. P. Wilson, third edition (Oxford University Press, 1970).

♥ I set up a toy area in a corner of every room in the house—even the bathroom. As she followed me from place to place, I always had a direction to steer her and something appropriate for her to do.

♥ When I feel the anger starting, I remind myself—out loud—that she isn't doing this just to get my goat!

♥   I eliminate all temptation. If the kitchen chairs are a problem, they go in the basement for a week. If she's climbing on the couch every five minutes, I pull the cushions off and put them on the floor. If she's using drawer handles as a ladder, I unscrew them. In a few days, she'll be attempting a different feat, and I can put everything back.

♥   *"You can help him to be independent by arranging the physical environment so he can do things for himself . . . [i.e.] toys on shelves at his level. . . ."*

—Family-support specialist Bernice Weissbourd in "Encouraging Independence," *Parents*, August 1989.

♥   I dressed him in simple clothing, fed him before he felt hunger pangs, and put him in for naps before exhaustion struck. He was a pleasure to be around as long as he was physically comfortable.

♥   We've cut back on visiting others for the time being. The constant chasing and scolding does nothing for either of our temperaments.

♥   *"The more you try to avoid conflict with your child by giving into immature demands, the greater the demands become. . . . In the long run, giving in leads to much more conflict with the child than you originally tried to avoid."*

—Ross Laboratories' *When Your Child is Difficult*, November 1983.

♥   We try not to hover. This creates tension and focuses too much attention on the forbidden object. You can be vigilant from half a room away.

♥   I resist the urge to lean on her in public for behavior that would be perfectly acceptable at home.

♥   When my baby demanded something, I used to verbalize the request. This gave me a minute to consider the consequences of complying versus refusing.

♥ I encouraged his attachment to a particular stuffed animal. His "security dog" seemed to help him resolve conflicts.

Gently Disciplining the Older Baby

♥ I don't try to squelch her tantrums. I let her get rid of the anger and then try to put into words for her whatever made her mad to begin with.

♥ When our baby's first word was "no," we realized how often we said it to him. After that, we'd make no comment about what he was doing wrong, but would suggest a substitute, like "you may play with the pots instead."

♥ *"The ideal thing, the perfect solution, would be to have sextuplets when you were in your early twenties. Then . . . you wouldn't find yourself in golden middle life still shouting, 'Don't run, please don't run! Not with that lollipop in your mouth.'"*

—Jean Kerr in *How I Got To Be Perfect* (Doubleday and Co., 1978).

♥ By making a game of his leading me to whatever he wants or needs, I've taught him to take my hand willingly when there's somewhere else *I* want *him* to be.

♥   I find that my words, tone, and facial expression must all match, no matter how "cute" her misbehavior may be. The slightest smile makes what I say meaningless.

♥   I didn't waste my breath giving warnings, since he wasn't capable of controlling himself. It was much better to wait till after the misbehavior occurred, when he could see for himself that I wouldn't accept it.

♥   I hug and sympathize with my daughter as I move her away, asking, "It's hard to be a baby, isn't it?"

♥   I keep a shoebox of intriguing things—a packet of coupons, an old trial-size shampoo bottle filled with water, crayons, and a coin purse—on top of the refrigerator. When the baby starts to get crazy, I settle her in the highchair and hand her the box. It's a guaranteed distraction.

♥   We always offer a simple explanation of why something isn't allowed. It seems to help her comply later, as though she understands that we have reasons for our rules.

♥   My baby's tantrums seemed to have a day-long effect on his mood. I used to hold him face-front till they were over, reminding him all the while that I didn't want him to hurt himself.

♥   I always allowed ten minutes more than I thought I needed to complete a task or activity which involved a baby. When I wasn't rushed, I had much more patience with their "detours."

♥   We avoid using the playpen as punishment. If it's used as a play area under normal circumstances, my baby likes it, but if he's dumped there in anger, he'll only scream his head off and make matters worse.

♥ We have a place—the top of the refrigerator—for anything that's used inappropriately. If he's trying to tear a book or stand on his music box, up they go. The same goes for anything thrown down the stairs or used as a weapon.

♥ If she had done something very wrong, I used to sit my daughter on a tiny stool facing a corner of the dining room. Young as she was, she still knew from my tone that I meant business.

♥ *"Wink at small faults—remember thou hast great ones."*
—Benjamin Franklin in *Poor Richard's Almanack* (Hallmark Editions, 1967)

8

Play

Parents of babies know how important playtime is to their little ones' sensory and muscle development (and later, to their verbal and social skills). However, it's not always easy to provide a play atmosphere and toys that will intrigue without overstimulating, and seem familiar without becoming boring. Special baby tactics can help you encourage play as both a solitary and a shared experience in an atmosphere appropriate to your baby's age, temperament, and activity level. This chapter provides tips from baby-care professionals and other parents on guiding and enriching a baby's play. Have fun!

INFANTS (Newborn to 8 Months)

What type of play does an infant need?

At first glance, infants do indeed live "the good life," with adult hands ready to meet their every need and with their days and nights a nonstop round of eat, sleep, and play. On closer inspection, however, their play is actually more like hard work than aimless frolic. From the start, the infant at play is busy exploring the world with each of her senses and with one body part after another. As she struggles to become more proficient, she is also developing motor and social skills along the way.

Though toy store shelves abound with toys labeled "Birth to 12 Months," it can be a mistake to immediately surround the newborn with dolls, busy boxes, and stacking rings. For many weeks, her parents are the only toys she really needs; making playthings a familiar part of an infant's environment before she's ready for them may well detract from their fascination when the right time comes.

Most babies are well into their third month before they unclench their fists, and won't hold even the lightest rattle until then! But long before, infants can watch and listen to you playing, as long as your hand and a bright object are within eight inches of their faces. As the weeks pass and they learn to follow the object with their eyes or lift their heads from a face-down position to watch you, they are more and more entertained by this kind of play.

At three months of age, an infant can grip that rattle at last, following its sound with her eyes as she moves it back and forth. Though she can't completely coordinate her eyes and hands until the second half of the year, all of this early play encourages the baby to work with both. But beware! Much as parents may wish to provide stimulation during a baby's alert moments, many little ones simply cannot handle the excitement. There's nothing wrong with leaving a wide-awake infant to her own devices for a while; in fact, she's apt to be just as happy watching you from across the room as when you're kneeling beside her—she can turn her head away or just close her eyes when she's had enough.

Nevertheless, most parents still look forward to the time when their babies will begin using toys to entertain themselves; after all, the more engrossing the activity, the freer mom and dad will feel to turn their attention to their own tasks. Presented with blocks, boxes, hoops, and other tools to practice their latest achievements in coordination, some babies may stay busy and contented for an hour; but most require some teaching. For these infants to enjoy playing alone, it may be up to their parents to get things started by introducing "playtime" as part of the daily routine.

It's a good idea to announce each playtime to your infant, and then sit with her for a while to demonstrate the toys you've set out. Then, as she becomes involved, step back and let her explore on her own. Frustrating as it may seem when, despite your careful planning, baby soon trails after you in search of entertainment, even a few minutes of concentration on baby's part can be considered a success at first. If these brief play periods are at all interesting, longer intervals will soon follow. And, with experimentation, you'll quickly learn what times of day are best, how many toys to set out, which ones frustrate, and which are the most appealing.

Play, be it alone or in company, is crucial to an infant's development. Safe, age-appropriate activities and the freedom to explore them offer the baby much more than a few minutes' amusement; they serve as a foundation for her developing intelligence, creativity, and a host of physical and verbal skills. The following techniques may help you as you plan the playtimes at your house:

Playing With a Restless or a Placid Infant

♥ I put my baby in the infant seat and place a large ball at his feet. He can cause it to roll toward me just by his natural kicking.

♥ Now that our son can sit by himself, we make use of roly-poly toys. Between the jingling bells and the bounce-back design, anything he does to them causes a reaction.

♥   When my daughter would start cranking and squirming, I'd get to her quickly, stand in her line of vision, and do an exact imitation of her sounds and actions. The interaction and attention always took care of her restlessness.

♥   I try to adjust my timing to my baby's, which usually means waiting with my "games" till after a feeding and then proceeding very slowly.

♥   *"Hang a colorful kite on the ceiling over the crib. It will catch your baby's eye, particularly when it moves in a gentle room breeze."*

> —Author and child development expert John J. Fisher in "Your Baby's First Playground," *Baby Talk*, February 1989.

♥   I always saw to it that his play efforts had an effect. Usually, a toy's squeaks, rattles, and bells were enough; but my smiles and claps acted as a payoff when the toy didn't offer its own response.

♥   I make sure I'm exactly at the baby's eye level. This has meant a lot of lying on the rug during the last six months, but he always pays attention this way.

♥   *"In church once, I was desperate for a quiet activity to amuse my restless son. I took off his sneaker, pulled the lace almost all the way out and, for the rest of the service, used lacing as entertainment."*

> —Children's writer Carole Forman, mother of three.

♥   I used to save the perfume-sample cards enclosed with department store bills and the scratch-and-sniff stickers that sometimes came home on my older boy's homework. My baby loved handling these.

♥   I tie colored yarn around my baby's wrists, sit her in my lap, and gently clap her hands together. When she tires of watching the strands floating around, I replace the yarn with a bell on a rubber band.

♥   I darken the room and turn on a flashlight. Then I try to get the baby to follow the beam with her eyes or pull off a blanket that I've thrown over the light.

♥   *"Seat or lay your baby on the end of a towel and pull her around the house. . . . Start slowly. With time and practice she'll learn to hang on and you can pick up the speed."*
> —*Today* show family physician Art Ulene, M.D., in *Bringing Out the Best in Your Baby* (MacMillan, 1986).

♥   We make tunnels by suspending the couch cushions between the coffee table and the couch itself, or by draping a blanket over a table. This really gets my daughter moving.

♥   To stimulate my daughter, I place her face-up on my knees and let her hang her head back. I pull her up by her arms and lay her back as many times as she wants to—she seems to like viewing the world from upside-down.

♥   I keep three teething rings in the refrigerator and a few more near the stove. Handing him two of them—a cold one and one that's just been resting above the pilot light—really gets him going.

Encouraging an Infant to Entertain Himself

♥   When he was very tiny, I kept the handle of his infant seat in the carrier position and tied on a rattle or two. He soon caught on that he could make them move by moving himself.

♥   I've always encouraged a nearby older sibling as entertainment. It seemed that by the baby's studying a child intent on an activity, he or she would, when the time came, naturally assume that same style of play.

♥   I vividly remember crawling on my hands and knees past his open bedroom door. I also faced his swing toward the window and the infant seat toward the TV—anything so he wouldn't see me and cry to be picked up.

♥   *"To keep themselves entertained they play musical chairs. I juggle them [the babies] between the playpens. . . ."*

—Ingrid Groller in "And Baby Makes Six," *Parents*, November 1988.

♥   I use the highchair the way you would a table and chairs for an older child. I give him unusual-feeling items like ice cubes, shredded paper, or a silky scarf and let him explore.

♥   From about five months of age until the baby could stand up, I used the crib as an extra play area. If I placed some toys around the perimeter before taking him out in the morning, he'd play for as long as forty-five minutes.

♥   My baby's toys have to be displayed attractively in order for her to get any real use from them. If the pieces aren't together or if the toys are scooped into a haphazard pile, she'll pick through them for a minute or two and then come looking for me.

♥   *"Reading the child is sometimes better than trusting the box [when selecting toys]; age appropriateness is sometimes wrong for a child in either direction."*

—Richard A. Weinberg, Ph.D., director, Center for Early Education and
Development, University of Minnesota-Minneapolis, in "Choosing
the Right Toys for Your Child," *Baby Talk*, October 1988.

♥   Tying ribbons to the covering grate of an oscillating fan and placing it on the nursery dresser top would keep my babies busy for quite a while as they alternated watching, kicking, and chewing on a toy.

♥   I cut the pictures of smiling babies from the sides of toy boxes and propped these "friends" around the sides of her crib.

♥   *"If you are going to use a [play]pen, the baby should become accustomed to it at 3 or 4 months, before he has learned to sit and crawl and before he has had the freedom of the floor."*

—Dr. Benjamin Spock in *Baby and Child Care* (Pocket Books, 1976).

♥   I fill a plastic soda bottle with about three inches of water, add some food coloring, cap it tightly, and let my baby roll it along the floor.

♥   We give our son an empty coffee can and a collection of items to drop inside. The different clanking sounds fascinate him.

♥   I put my daughter in the highchair with a few strips of masking tape and some lightweight toys. Then I could probably leave town and she wouldn't notice.

OLDER BABIES (9 to 15 Months)

What can play teach the older baby?

Once a baby becomes mobile, her surroundings will seem very new to her. She gains a fresh perspective by spending so much of her time upright, since many items and activities that went unnoticed from her position on the rug or in the infant seat are now at eye level. She can look out the window and follow you from room to room. She's attracted to anything out of the ordinary, be it a basket of laundry in the hall or the pile of books awaiting a trip to the library.

Just as they did as infants, older babies learn by observing the activities of other family members. They'll play at whatever *you* make look interesting, even if it's only changing bedsheets; and, as they become more confident and more mobile, will wander off to explore elsewhere, using you as home base.

This new-found desire to roam may keep a baby busier than before, but it has its drawbacks as well. Along with access to every room in the house, a mobile baby gains entry into the world of frustration. She's apt to get herself into some unusual predicaments while at play, unable to extricate herself from beneath the rocking chair or from inside a cabinet. She is baffled and angered when her attempts to open a box, fit pieces together, or keep her ball atop a table repeatedly meet with failure. And what's more, she has to get used to being denied some intriguing-looking items because of their potential for danger.

You can usually figure out what has piqued your baby's interest just by watching her in action. Fortunately for parents, babies of this age are still easily distracted and nearly always willing to accept substitutions; this allows you to divert her from danger or frustration without actually directing her activities. Allowing a baby to set the tone and pace of her own playtimes fosters curiosity, self-esteem, and her growing independence.

When you do play together, you'll find that the older baby enjoys practicing newly mastered skills as much now as in infancy. Offering nesting toys, containers with lids, and other more intricate items will provide valuable practice stacking, twisting, filling, and dumping. At the same time, you can appeal to her blossoming social side by encouraging her to dance and make music, play hide and seek, use a toy phone, or pretend with dolls.

As she grows, most of the older baby's learning will be done through imitation and play. She'll benefit most when that playtime is spent with items that are simple enough to spark creativity and versatile enough to grow with her. Tempting as toy catalogs may be, it's neither practical nor necessary to purchase new toys for every stage of her development. Hunting around the house for common objects to use in new ways (a sleeve of plastic cups, for example, or tennis balls in a cupcake pan) can achieve the same purpose.

When you do go toy shopping, keep the enduring classics in mind. It's no accident that some of the 1950s' favorites are still on toy store shelves! And when you're ready to make your selection, remember that the right toy can serve as both a plaything and as valuable exposure to the unknown. Consider a farm set for the city baby, or a toy ship for one who lives far inland.

In the end, there is no right or wrong way for a baby to play, for each has her own style. But it's up to the parents to provide the atmosphere and the tools. Here are some suggestions to help you encourage and guide your baby:

Enriching the Older Baby's Playtime

♥   I place three distinctly shaped toys on drawing paper and trace around the edges. Then we practice matching the toy to its shape.

♥   By doing our ball-playing in a hallway with all doors closed, I can increase my son's accuracy and enjoyment.

♥   We shop for toys that, with a little imagination, can be used in different ways. His favorite is a small dollhouse that also works as a fire station, a school, and a store.

♥   Very often, I would involve our cat in our play. Roll her a ball, toss her a treat, hold out a hand to pet her—her reactions were immediate and predictable and so very exciting to my son.

♥   I sit him on the kitchen floor with a four-inch wash basin filled with oatmeal. Once a few bowls, cups, and spoons are added, it's our indoor sandbox.

♥   By the time my first child was a year old, I'd already given up on keeping her take-apart toys intact. This time around, I keep a lost-and-found box on the baby's dresser for any stray pieces I come across. He still drops toys in the wastebasket now and then, but when he drags out the stacking rings, we can usually come up with all of them.

♥   *"Make sure you're both having fun. If you're not enjoying yourself, it's a safe bet that your baby isn't having much fun either."*
     —Margaret L. Agoglia in "What's So Funny?" *Baby Talk*, February 1990.

♥   I encourage him to use toys as miniature versions of my household tools. When I vacuum, for example, he's right next to me with his corn popper.

♥   We gave the baby an eight-inch plastic pail with a handle. Depending on where her imagination is taking her that day, her pail serves as her briefcase, lunch box, purse, or suitcase.

♥   I gave my son an old, easy-to-open pocketbook. I fill it with all kinds of gadgets—keys, a hairbrush, a plastic hammer, an eggbeater—and work on teaching him how each item is used.

♥   I invite a friend and her baby over and turn the little ones loose with a basin of water, a pile of leaves, or some homemade modeling dough.

♥   *"In the second year the best buy is a low stable toy on swivel castors which he can sit on and push along with the feet. . . . Large-scale toys to push or pull are [also] a 'must.'"*
—Penelope Leach in *Your Baby and Child* (Alfred A. Knopf, 1989).

♥   We cut photos of familiar objects from magazines, mount them on heavy paper, and try to match them with their real-life counterparts. My daughter loves this three-dimensional lotto game. (The original lotto game had the child match cards bearing pictures, letters, or numbers with similar figures on a board.)

♥   A gym-teacher friend gave us an old three-wheel scooter board from his school. We use it indoors in every way imaginable, both for exercise and just for fun.

♥   I included my son's stuffed animals in many of our activities. Watching me pretend with toys paved the way for his own fantasy play.

Helping the Older Baby Enjoy Solitary Play

♥   When she's playing happily, I resist the urge to interrupt with comments, suggestions, or even eye contact. Doing so breaks the spell.

♥ We provide a lot of water play, for here the baby can move at his own pace, use his imagination, and be virtually free of frustration.

♥ Whether he's in the playpen or on the floor, I don't offer a lot of toys. My son plays much more intently when he has only three or four items in front of him.

♥ *"If you have friends with small children, suggest trading toys and books. By the time your own child's things get back, they'll be interesting once more."*
—Brooke McKamy Beebe in *Best Bets for Babies* (Dell Publishing Co., 1981).

♥ We're lucky enough to have a toy library in our area. This is a great way to provide my daughter with playthings that may be perfect for the level she's at today, but would quickly become boring.

♥ I bought a set of plastic links which I used to attach toys to the stroller, shopping cart, highchair, and playpen. When each of my babies was at the toy-tossing stage, they were kept busy retrieving their own things.

♥   *"Collect thirty or forty small objects of different sizes and shapes in some sort of large container, and you will have a homemade toy that will keep a child occupied for long periods of time. They are fascinated by collections of small interesting objects."*

> —Child psychologist Burton L. White in *The First Three Years of Life* (Prentice-Hall, 1975).

♥   My baby has a rather large toy collection, thanks mainly to gifts and hand-me-downs. To keep her from getting tired of them, I divided her toys into three boxes and stashed two of them in the closet. Now she has access to only one group of toys per month.

♥   My baby is so intrigued by his older sister's toys that I keep her room off limits. But when I want him to amuse himself, I pull a few of her things out into the hall for him. It does the trick every time.

♥   I used to make an activity disappear at the first sign of my babies' boredom or frustration. If the activity was put away on a positive note, they were more likely to be excited by it next time.

♥   I keep silent and make whatever I'm doing seem pretty boring. My son comes looking for me quite often, but soon wanders off in search of better entertainment.

♥   I designated an old magazine as hers and browsed through it with her. Now, when I need a few minutes, I hand it to her to use in any way she wants. She enjoys the familiar pictures so much that she's surprisingly gentle with her "buk."

♥   We save small boxes and containers from soap, toothpaste, butter, candy, yogurt, and so on. Now that she's past the gnawing stage, she'll play with these and a paper bag for an hour.

♥ We have one cabinet in the kitchen and another in the family room that are all his. Emptying, switching, playing with, and replacing the contents keeps him quite busy.

♥ When I introduced a new activity, I set it up at my feet the first day, near the doorway the second day, and in the hall the third day, gradually moving the baby farther off by himself.

"*Here are the numbers for our car phone, the restaurant, the movies, and the neighbor next door, or you can fax us at.....*"

9

Babysitters and Caregivers

---

*Most of today's busy parents use childcare
in one form or another; and no matter
whether the caretaker is a doting
grandma or a center serving dozens of
children, the relationship between your
baby and his caregiver is extremely
important. There are certain baby tactics
that can help you make the best
arrangements possible for the care of your
infant while encouraging a special bond
with his caregiver, or, for an older baby,
can help you handle his separation
anxiety and plan for a worry-free day or
evening away from him. This chapter
offers you the solutions used by parents
and specialists to deal with their own
childcare problems. May your hours away
be guilt-free!*

INFANTS (Newborn to 8 Months)

***What special problems might you encounter when using a
babysitter or caregiver?***

As a new parent, you may find that opinions on the ad-
visability of using childcare for your infant are sharply divided. Citing the importance of the early one-to-one
relationship between parent and baby, some child-rearing experts suggest that at least one parent remain by an infant's
side for the first six weeks (or six months, or the whole year,
depending on the speaker). But just as many others insist that
if sitters are introduced before a baby reaches that fourth-
month awareness of mother over others, he'll form healthy
attachments to them and, used to interacting with several
people from the start, become an even more competent and
sociable preschooler.

Naturally, each set of parents must make its own decisions
regarding how and when to begin using childcare. The least
problematic babysitting setup, of course, is that which involves relatives, close friends, or others with strong emotional
ties to the family; but these arrangements are more often the
exception than the rule. You can be at ease with another

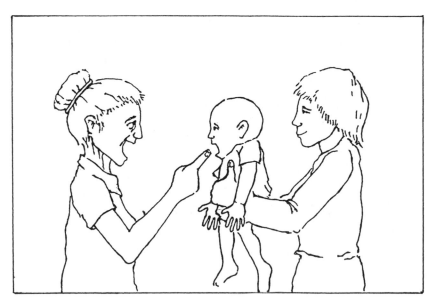

choice if you've carefully researched your options and considered the difficulties you may encounter along the way.

The one-to-one care so ideal for infants is extremely expensive to use on a long-term basis. And no matter what you pay your sitters, you must still cope with back-up care in case of the sitter's illness, differences in method and philosophy, and trust in everything from their commitment to your baby to their unsupervised presence in your home. With group arrangements, you must also face the possibilities of over-stimulation, delays in meeting your baby's needs, personnel shifts, lost belongings, and the appropriateness of an infant "curriculum."

Daycare facilities and their standards vary widely, as do past clients' opinions of the individual babysitters you might interview. In addition to checking references, it's probably best to set your own criteria and then visit several times beforehand in order to let your instincts guide you. Glowing recommendations aside, does the setup *feel* right? Does he/she instantly warm up to your baby and seem at ease handling him? If other children are present, do they seem contented? Bear in mind that an infant has a characteristic way of dealing with new surroundings that can be anything from solemn observation, to excited gurgles, to abject misery. Though it's sometimes suggested that parents line up childcare even before the baby is born, his temperament should figure as a crucial factor in your decision.

Some parents are uncomfortable about (or resent) their infant forming a close bond to his caregiver. But actually, this is a sign that your baby feels safe and comfortable with the person you've hired. As long as you're satisfied that this will be a fairly long-term commitment, a strong infant/sitter attachment should actually put many of your childcare worries to rest.

Whatever your feelings about entrusting the care of your infant to others, you should remember that helping him establish a degree of independence is part of a parent's job. Choosing someone special to help with his care benefits all three of you. Here are some ideas to help you make the childcare arrangements best suited to your family:

Encouraging a Healthy Bond Between Caregiver and Infant

♥   For the first eight or nine months, I exchanged sitting favors with a cousin I'm very close to. Besides watching each other's babies, we also socialized frequently, so her presence in my home was very familiar to my son.

♥   We always asked our sitters to come forty-five minutes early and, during the time we were still home, would have them do most of the baby-handling. This extra step seemed to reassure the baby and was easier on us as well.

♥   My baby and I occasionally stop at the babysitter's house during nonworking days, and I encourage her to drop in on us. The more social our relationship, the more natural her interaction with my baby will be.

♥   *"Spend lots of casual, unrushed time with your caregiver and baby so the baby gets the message that this new person is a friend. . . ."*

—Mother of two Freddi Greenberg, editor-in-chief, *Child* magazine.

♥   I encouraged my sitter to take the baby to playgroup, the park, and other group situations where the baby would have to turn to her for reassurance or comfort.

♥   I buy for my home some of the same playthings the baby uses at daycare. This helps to downplay the difference between her two environments.

♥   At day's end, *"Don't rush to take your baby; wait until she gives some clue that she's ready—a smile, a shy stare, a body move in your direction. . . ."*

Nancy Balaban, Ed.D., in "Goodbyes Without Tears," *Working Mother*, January 1989.

♥   We invite my sitter and her husband to brunch or dinner about once a month. It's good for my son to interact with the sitter in our home as well as in hers.

♥   At pick-up time each day, we hang around the daycare center for ten or fifteen minutes to avoid giving the baby the idea that it's a place I want to rush away from.

♥   If her grandparents weren't able to babysit, I didn't go out. This way, bonding, trust, and guilt were never factors.

♥   I keep pictures of my son's babysitter in our house. This gives me opportunities to mention her on days when he won't be seeing her.

♥   *"Have the sitter introduce a new toy that you've stashed just for this occasion. Or if a special treat . . . is on the agenda, have the babysitter offer it."*

—Brooke McKamy Beebe in *Best Bets for Babies* (Dell Publishing Co., 1981).

♥   We avoided confusion on the baby's part by using the same sitter, and only that sitter, for as many months as possible. If he or she was unavailable on a particular occasion, we took the baby with us.

♥   I provide my sitter with a notebook in which to make notes about the day's meals, naps, diaper changes, problems, etc. This keeps her completely focused on the baby's schedule, makes me feel more a part of things, and eliminates the "reporting time" at the end of the day.

♥   I looked and looked till I found a childcare setup I was completely at ease with. Now there's very little tension or guilt for my baby to pick up on.

Making Babysitting Arrangements for an Infant

♥   When I placed an ad for a babysitter, I'd save time by first interviewing all callers on the phone. Then I'd check the references of my top three candidates before inviting them to my home. This way, the only thing left to do during the in-person interview was to watch how they handled my baby.

♥   Rather than pick someone close to home, I use a babysitter who lives a quarter of a mile from my job. I have extra time with my baby during our "commute," and I can be at her side in five minutes if something goes wrong.

♥   My rule is, the younger the baby, the older the sitter should be. For now, I'll only use someone who's a parent themselves; but an energetic high-schooler will be perfect once my son is walking and talking.

♥   To find out what a potential sitter would do in emergencies and matters of discipline, I bring up six or seven hypothetical situations during our interview and ask, point-blank, how she'd handle them.

♥   *"When you interview prospective family daycare providers . . . [consider] whom else in the family your child will come in contact with each day. Be sure to meet them."*
    —Phyllis LaFarge in "A Family Day-Care Checklist," *Parents*, January 1990.

♥   We presented each sitter we interviewed with a detailed, written job description. Their reactions to that single piece of paper told us a lot about their levels of competence and commitment.

"Have you sat for us before?"

♥   We advertised for a "grandmotherly type" and offered her three set mornings a week, regardless of whether I'd be out or at home during those hours. By offering a fixed schedule, it was easy to find a top-quality person.

♥   I get my sitters through a very reputable school for nannies. They cost a little more, but a thorough background check has already been done and I'm assured of their training, experience, and commitment.

♥   *"During the early months, we felt comfortable using someone our babies didn't know well. As the babies grew more aware, though, we made sure our nighttime babysitter was someone whose face they'd recognize if they woke unexpectedly."*

—Early childhood teacher Diane Crisci, mother of two.

♥   I started a Working Moms' Network in my office building. Our biweekly meetings offer support and ideas to group members and an organized, united front to our bosses.

♥   When checking references, I bear in mind that applicants will only offer names of those who'll speak highly of them. Asking specific, pointed questions of these references, like "What were her strengths and weaknesses?" or "How frequently was she late/absent?" results in much more information than does "What did you think of her?"

♥   When touring a daycare facility, *"Don't be fooled by the quality of the decor or the number of new Fisher-Price toys on the shelf. What is important is how it feels. If you can feel the warmth, then sign up. . . ."*

—Christopher Green, M.D., in *Dr. Green's Baby Book* (Fawcett Columbine, 1988).

♥   After calling the guidance office of a junior high school that's within walking distance of my home, I got eight calls from students interested in babysitting.

♥   I put a lot of faith in my son's reactions. If a particular sitter makes him act anxious or fearful in a different way than usual, I assume that the person is either too aloof or too overbearing with him and do not call them again.

♥   Three close friends and I took turns watching each other's infants. An afternoon alone with three babies could sometimes get a bit crazy, but the two afternoons I earned in exchange were definitely worth it.

OLDER BABIES (9 to 15 Months)

How does the childcare situation change as baby begins his second year?

At nine through twelve months of age, most babies are extremely attached to their primary caregiver, whether it be a parent or a sitter. As they gradually discover freedom of movement, babies still demand to be held (or will clutch at a familiar leg) when they see that special person preparing to leave the room, or when others walk in. This is not the best time to alter childcare arrangements, because no matter whether a baby is already accustomed to daycare or has had mommy at his side since birth, he's not going to be too happy about a change.

Fortunately, you can expect some of this clinginess to abate at around thirteen months of age. In fact, many babies become downright sociable at this point, voluntarily approaching others for a pat or to offer a toy. And, though they're still apt to protest vigorously when you leave, babies of fourteen or fifteen months begin to understand that you *will* come back for them when they're left in someone else's care.

Strangely enough, some older babies cry just as loudly upon their parent's return as they do when that parent leaves them. Though this may seem like a deliberate attempt to change your mind about leaving in the future, babies of this age aren't that manipulative! This heart-rending behavior is more likely a release of pent-up feelings, showing that the baby feels safest "letting go" in your presence. And usually, a baby who cries when his parents come and go can be quickly distracted. (His contentment during the course of your absence is really more important.)

The older baby's emerging physical skills mean that he now requires space to move about freely and safely. This is not the time to leave him in the care of someone who regards house-keeping as a top priority or who looks after more than four children without assistance. Your now-mobile baby requires a watchful eye and a fairly relaxed attitude toward the mess left by his explorations! He is likely to become a bit territorial about toys and, at this age, delights in verbal stimulation, so he'll probably do best someplace where he'll find plenty of both!

When introducing or changing an older baby's childcare setup, some advance preparation may help. You might wish to enroll him in a playgroup or library storytime beforehand for practice interacting with other adults. Having the sitter make a few advance visits (or stopping in at the daycare home/ center several times) will help the new arrangement become more familiar. It's best to hold off on any other changes in a baby's routine while he's adjusting to daycare or a sitter; and above all, don't rush things! You'll feel most comfortable if you're sure he's contented while you're away.

When all is said and done, older babies are still ruled by "wants"; and what they want is for you to be within close range every minute of the day! This is impossible in many cases and highly improbable in all the rest, so find a setting that meets your expectations and requirements, kiss him goodbye, and go!

Remember, millions of babies before yours have emerged triumphant from their hours in someone else's care. Here's what worked for some of their parents:

Easing an Older Baby's Separation Fears

♥ I would tell my son I was leaving in a few minutes, then get him and the babysitter busy at something before making a quiet exit. If he didn't witness my departure, it didn't bother him nearly as much.

♥   I have a set "goodbye" routine that involves mentioning what she'll play with that morning, eat for lunch, and do with me later in the day. Then I collect some advance kisses for naptime. This helps put some order in her day—at least for me.

♥   I use an alarm clock to signal my departure. This almost makes it seem like someone else's idea, so my son doesn't get as angry with me.

♥   *"If you sneak off, you may save yourself a crisis at the time, but you create an anxious child, wondering when the next desertion will occur . . ."*
             —Dr. T. Berry Brazelton in *What Every Baby Knows* (Addison-Wesley, 1987).

♥   When I left my baby, I always told him exactly when he'd see me again, like "after lunch" or "after naptime." I asked my sitter to repeat this several times during the time she was with him so he'd begin to understand that I *did* come back when I said I would.

♥   I bring my child to work with me every now and then so that she can better understand where I go and what I'm doing when I have to leave her.

♥   *"I gave him something of mine—jewelry or a scarf smelling of my cologne, a picture of me, anything that he could hold until I got back . . . a little of me, in a sense."*
             —Gladys A. Blose of The Family Resource Center in Northport.

♥   Each time I return home, I sing Hap Palmer's reassuring "Mommy Comes Back." My baby recognizes the song from his "Baby Songs" videotape, and having it acted out in person affirms my earlier promise to return to him.

♥   We bring in the sitter after my daughter's asleep for the night. Since she has never awakened in the eight months we've been doing this, we feel safe enjoying an evening out while she's none the wiser.

♥   We're very consistent about which of us drops off and picks up our son and about the time this will take place. He's reassured by the "sameness."

♥   With the permission of my daycare center, I started my son a week earlier than I needed to and stayed with him for steadily decreasing periods of time: six hours the first day, then four, then two, then one, and finally a half hour. By that last day, we both felt at home with his new routine.

♥   *"I made my thirteen-month-old a little book called 'Stephanie Goes to Daycare.' It showed everything from getting up in the morning to saying bye-bye at daycare, with pictures of the kids she would play with and the activities she would be doing. . . . Because she was pre-verbal, I think the book helped her identify her feelings and get over the sadness of separation much more quickly."*

—Columnist, writer, and editor Sandi Kahn Shelton, mother of three.

♥   I made a videotape of myself doing some ordinary things around the house while talking and singing to my son. My sitter plays it for him at lunchtime, and I like to think it helps break up the ten-hour separation we foist on the baby every work day.

♥   We all suffered less when my husband dropped the baby off. For some reason, my son would offer only mild protest on those days, compared to absolute hysterics when I left him.

"Mom's home!"

♥   I get to the daycare center early enough to linger for ten minutes or so, making sure I spend those minutes on the fringes having coffee or chatting with another mother. This way I sort of ease away.

Ensuring That All Goes Well in the Parents' Absence

♥   We first hired a young girl as a mother's helper for the summer. By the time I began to leave her alone with the baby, she'd already been around so often that she knew our routine completely.

♥   Every now and then I either come home early or stop at home unexpectedly during the day. Finding everything under control long before I'm supposed to show up is very reassuring.

♥   *"Have the sitter come a half hour before you're leaving, to plan which favorite activity the child and the sitter can do while mommy is gone (play in a sink full of water, make a tape recording, etc.)"*

> —Advertising-agency partner and writer Bonnie Mitelman, mother of three.

♥   I ask my sitter to bring some of her own things—crayons, books, toys—to my house. Anything that's new and different will keep my baby busier while I'm gone.

♥   When I'm using a new babysitter, I always ask a friend to "drop over" and call me with a report on what's happening at my house.

♥   I call home twice a day, at previously agreed-upon times, for a full report. Since the sitter expects my calls, I never feel that I'm interrupting things.

♥   I use a thirteen-year-old neighbor whose parents only permit her to babysit when they're available to help out with emergencies.

♥ *"I stayed home the first couple of times and dilly-dallied around, listening from another room for consistent and loving feedback."*

—Psychotherapist Debra Pitman, D.S.W., mother of two.

♥ We keep a laminated list of emergency phone numbers taped to the refrigerator door and, realizing that most junior high kids don't carry cab fare, clip a ten-dollar bill to it each time we go out.

♥ I offer the sitter a simple chart showing the baby's current likes and dislikes, routine and problem behaviors. This helps her stay two steps ahead of him.

♥ We encourage certain liberties while we're gone, to make the time spent with a sitter almost like a party: water play, coloring with chalk, special snacks, a Raffi videotape, etc.

♥ *"I left a whole bucket of activities which I'd prepared ahead of time, with very specific instructions on when and how the babysitter was to use them."*

—Early childhood teacher Mary Ann Parsons, mother of three.

♥ I hand each caregiver a very detailed copy of my baby's daily routine. Some may deviate from it more than others, but I feel better having told them what she normally does at that time of day.

♥ We always asked our sitters to come after all the baby chores were done. It was a relief to know that their only responsibility was to entertain her—so much less could go wrong this way.

♥ Every babysitter gets a complete tour of our house, during which we point out all the potential trouble spots for the baby. This may seem like overkill, but our obvious concern leads to some extra vigilance on the sitter's part.

10
Car Travel

Car travel can pose a problem to parents of babies, if only because the baby's frequent and varied complaints while on the road seem then to be magnified by her proximity to the rest of the family! To make plans for and survive a car trip with an infant, or to properly pack for and execute a drive with an older baby, you will need dependable baby tactics. This chapter will provide you with those car-travel problem-solving techniques that have worked for experts and other parents. Happy motoring!

INFANTS (Newborn to 9 Months)

Why do many infants dislike car travel?

With the exception of the journey home from the hospital, new parents often spend the first weeks of their baby's life relatively house bound. Doctors' "shelter-her-from-the-public" orders aside, there's something about strapping a floppy, helpless newborn into a car seat and exposing her to traffic woes that invites a shudder!

But before too long, mothers and fathers become anxious to rejoin the rest of the world, and car travel often figures largely in their plans. The infant isn't likely to share their restlessness, however, and so may not prove a willing participant in a planned family drive. (Though most newborns nod off at the start of the engine and nap peacefully for the ride's duration, this tendency fades as they become more aware of their surroundings.)

For one thing, car rides are apt to bring into play an infant's natural fears about changes in her environment: traffic noises, scenery flitting by the window, and the confusion of so many people strapped into such close quarters can be most upsetting.

Car rides can cause an infant physical discomfort as well, due to such things as over- or underdressing, the lack of support offered by a too-spacious carseat, the sun in her eyes, or elevation-related ear popping. It's also possible that she dislikes her rear-facing position that, in effect, causes her to endure an entire drive in reverse.

In addition, car rides can pose scheduling problems for your baby. At times, the weather, road work, or police activity can jam up even the most open road. Unanticipated or unavoidable delays like these can mean that your infant gets a late feeding, sleeps when you don't want her to, or worst of all, screams in abject misery for thirty minutes rather than the ten to which you'd resigned yourself!

For a car ride—even a two-minute drive to a store—to proceed with all possible smoothness, it's up to the parent to plan ahead. Keeping an infant's natural impatience in mind, try to depart when the roads are least crowded. Every bumper-to-bumper minute you save will count in your favor! Before leaving, consider your baby's personal state as well. She'll feel most agreeable when she's just been rested, fed, and changed. Even if you don't plan to leave the car, always bring along a well-stocked diaper bag. The best-laid plans have been known to change!

Finally, remember that infants are happiest when they can see you. Strapping the car seat up front allows you to give your baby the attention she craves even while you're driving. Here are some more hints to help make family car rides more a pleasure than an ordeal:

Preparing for a Drive With an Infant

♥ I made to-do and to-pack checklists and tacked them inside the hall closet for last-minute reviews each time I left for a drive with my baby. This lessened the chance of forgetting something vital.

♥ If the ride was to be a long one, we tried to leave with a still-sleeping baby at 4:30 A.M. (If she stirred, a quick feeding and lots of blankets usually lulled her back to sleep.) By the time she was truly awake and fidgety, we were several hours into the trip.

Baby in neutral

♥   We start a long drive at 6 P.M. The baby usually starts to complain after about forty-five minutes, so then we feed her, play with her, and pray for her to fall asleep for the night.

♥   My first baby was usually left at home when I did errands, but she's now a busy grade-schooler and my car trips around town have tripled. The fact that our new baby's been in the car since Day One helped us avoid the awful breaking-in period we eventually went through with our oldest.

♥   *"Remember that your objective is to get there safely and happily. If your objective is to get there* soon, *you might be foregoing 'safely,' and you will surely forego 'happily.' "*

> —Parenting expert Vicki Lansky in *Traveling With Your Baby* (Bantam Books, 1985).

♥   If the baby's going to be riding with me, I plan my errand or schedule my appointment so that we leave at his naptime. He sleeps, and I enjoy a peaceful drive.

♥   I start a drive immediately after my son's nap and feeding so I'm guaranteed he'll be alert for an hour or so. I don't want to waste any of his precious sleep-time in the car!

♥   *"When [the rest of the family] sets off, [travel writer Martha Shirk] and her baby are nowhere to be found. That's because they are on a plane, jetting off to meet the [others] at their final destination."*

> —Writer and editor Jody Gaylin in "Car Trip Survival Guide," *Parents*, May 1990.

♥   My baby's three-hour feeding schedule doesn't allow much time for errands. But if I lay out everything I'll need the night before—jackets, keys, purse, diaper bag, etc.—we can be in the car in less than two minutes.

♥   In case of car trouble, we've stashed a diaper, a bottle of sterile water, and a restaurant pack of breadsticks in the glove compartment.

♥ I kept a "car bag" stocked with bib, spoon, diapers, wipes, toys, a blanket, and a change of clothes. We could leave for a drive at a moment's notice, because all I needed to pack was her bottle.

♥ *"Avoid letting [baby] travel on too full . . . a stomach and always make sure that you have cloths to mop up if accidents occur."*

—John Cobb, M.D., in *Babyshock* (Prentice Hall, 1983).

♥ In the event of an emergency, we keep a few dollars' worth of quarters and a list of important phone numbers in an envelope under the floor mat.

♥ I invested ahead of time in several toys—two clip-on busy boxes, a push-button guitar, and a long-playing music box—to be used only in the car.

♥ My Sunday paper has a column detailing all local road work for the upcoming week. I save this page so that we can plan our travel routes around construction.

Surviving a Car Trip With an Infant

♥ I was always carsick as a child, and I recall that being able to see out the windows was helpful. So just in case, I keep my baby's seat elevated and up front.

♥ When our son is awake and content in his car seat, we reward him with talk and play. This should help him associate riding in the car with fun.

♥ I tape pictures of babies to the car door and the back of the front seat. They're much more interesting to look at than blue vinyl!

♥ For a do-it-yourself snack that lasts the whole trip, I tie a bagel to her car seat with a shoelace.

♥   *"I cover the back seat and floor with large towels, so feedings in the car won't be as messy."*

> —Port Washington Parent Resource Center's Trudy Hoffman, Associate "Mommy-and-Me" Coordinator.

♥   We don't hesitate to drive several miles off the highway for rest stops. We can usually find a grassy area in which to set the baby free, something we could never do in a roadside fast-food place.

♥   *"If the car is roomy enough and you don't mind the extra responsibility, bring along the kids' favorite babysitter."*

> —Ellyce Field and Susan Shlom in *Kids and Cars* (Melius and Peterson Publishing Corporation, 1988).

♥   I keep the baby's seat in the middle of the rear seat. It's safer, and we avoid the worst of the glaring sunlight.

♥   We put a rolled-up receiving blanket on either side of the baby to keep him upright in the car seat, and another under his knees to avoid pressure from the crotch strap.

♥   My baby becomes uneasy when we drive in the dark, so I open the glove compartment for an instant night light.

♥   I found a convex mirror which attaches to the visor and gives me a clear view of the entire backseat. Now I have an easier time solving baby crises before they get out of hand.

♥   *"Without a doubt you will run into those moments when Timmy simply refuses to entertain himself. . . . Just tell your spouse very insistently that it's your turn to drive."*

—Sanford and Joan Portnoy in *How to Take Great Trips With Your Kids* (Harvard Common Press, 1983).

♥   I encouraged my older children to take turns entertaining the baby. The uninterrupted interaction was good for all of them.

♥   I tied a small stuffed rabbit to a piece of elastic and hung it on the garment hook. The motion of the car sent it bouncing right into the baby's line of vision.

♥   We make a "car mobile" by hooking a bungee cord, complete with rattles and small toys, between the front-seat headrests.

OLDER BABIES (9 to 15 Months)

Why does a settled-down passenger begin her rebellion anew?

At some point during infancy, most babies become more accepting of a ride in the car. Wide-eyed and contented, they are soothed by the engine's hum and whatever music you provide. And once they reach that twenty-pound mark that enables you to face their seats forward, most find the sights along the road quite entertaining. But you're not out of the woods yet! As any parent who's ever tried to get a rigid, screaming one-year-old into a car seat can tell you, you're likely to encounter varying degrees of resistance at different points throughout babyhood.

An older baby is still very much attuned to her physical state. She'll let you know in no uncertain terms when the car is too noisy, too bumpy, too hot, or too breezy to suit her. And as she becomes more social, a baby is quickly bored when her parents pay more attention to the road and their own conversation than to playing with her. The same old roadside scenery begins to lose appeal, too; particularly at night when the only things she can see are street and traffic lights.

But she finds her confinement even more frustrating. A baby is happiest when she can roam and explore, but she's forced by the car seat's tethers and crossbar to sit practically motionless for what must seem like forever. A toy or snack may buy you some time, but any time you drive for more than a few minutes, she'll probably make her wish to be set free quite clear.

Babies of a year or more may begin to equate a car ride with something at the trip's end that they find unpleasant. For example, if a baby hates stores, is miserable at the babysitter's house, or has recently accompanied you on a seemingly endless four-hour trip, you can count on her to revolt if you so much as pick up your keys. Once she's strapped in, though, she's likely to be calmed by the motion of the car . . . until you dare to stop at a light or slow down in traffic.

You can hope for time to bring change; meanwhile, it's probably wise to keep drives brief and to a minimum until your baby puts this phase behind her. On necessary trips, books, stuffed animals, or an adult in close proximity can provide welcome diversion. When the going gets particularly rough, or when you plan to drive any distance, you might wish to try some of these ideas:

Packing for a Drive With an Older Baby

♥   A two-handled plastic grocery bag, hung from the passenger door and with a roll of paper towels inside, is a great help in keeping the car clean.

♥   I always take along a jug of water and some plastic cups. It's cheaper and easier than making a stop at the store, and spills are no big deal.

♥   *"We composed a list of absolute necessities. . . . After learning the hard way, we swore that we would follow the list for all outings longer than ten minutes."*

> —Toni Sands Barrass in "Have Baby, Will Travel," *American Baby,* July 1989.

♥   After surviving a few disasters, we now *pack* the outfit the baby will wear at our destination. Any old shirt will do for the drive itself.

♥   We kept a medicine box containing Band-Aids, antiseptic, syrup of ipecac, and acetaminophen under the seat of the car.

♥   I put a deep basket next to his car seat and stuffed a blanket in the bottom before adding toys. This way, everything was within the baby's reach.

♥   Before long drives, my friend and I lend each other a bag of our baby's toys. Unfamiliar playthings translate into quiet miles.

♥   *"For car snacks, I always bring the plainest, cleanest, most unappealing food possible."*

> —Writer Linda Lague, mother of two, in "Driving Controls," Good Housekeeping and Sesame Street Magazine's *Kids of Summer 1990.*

♥   Snacks keep my baby busy in the car, of course, but also throw off his eating schedule. I compromise by packing something that can pass as a meal, like string cheese, Cheerios, and raisins.

♥   I make sure to pack for a drive when my baby is elsewhere. This guarantees that everything I pull from my "bag of tricks" will be a novelty.

♥   We always brought along a penlight with batteries. It came in handy both as a tool and a toy.

♥   When we take a drive, we leave the ruffly dresses and lace tights at home. Instead, we dress the baby in a comfortable, wrinkle-free, one-piece outfit and pack a second for emergency changes.

♥   I keep a deflated beach ball and a few balloons in my trunk to play with during exercise breaks along the way.

♥   If we're taking a cooler with us, I throw in one or two frozen teething rings. They have the same soothing effect as a snack but don't spoil the baby's appetite.

♥   We used to take along a set of old, just-scrubbed keys on a ring. This fascinated my babies like no toy ever did.

Avoiding a Revolt on the Road

♥   We found an extra-high bed tray which fits across her car seat. She finds it much easier to entertain herself now that there's a flat surface to play on.

♥   A receiving blanket, closed into the window, keeps the sun out of the baby's eyes and lets him play hide-and-seek when he gets bored.

Kum-ba-ya, Lord, kum-ba-ya"

♥   We keep preschool toy catalogs on hand for fussy times. She can manage them by herself, and her fascination with the pictures buys us some valuable time.

♥   *"Sing 'Kum-ba-ya' at the top of your lungs and keep driving! They will pass out eventually."*
>—Writer and editor Marion Winik, mother of two.

♥   I used to beg, borrow, or steal used pop-up and lift-and-look books. They almost always needed repair after a long ride, but they kept my babies occupied.

♥   Offering my son a clean window and a plastic bowl of Colorforms usually guarantees at least fifteen minutes of quiet.

♥   *"You can make a leisurely meal in the car take up to a half an hour—if you're clever."*
>—Writer Rhonda Barfield, mother of three, in "The Art of Weekend Visiting," *Baby Talk*, November 1989.

♥   If a baby was along for the ride, I abandoned any plans to enjoy the scenery or talk to my husband. Car travel was much less stressful if I assumed the role of entertainer/food dispenser from the moment we left the driveway.

♥   I taped over the "Volume" dial on a hand-held cassette player and invested in a sturdy pair of headphones. On long drives, I pop in a cassette, pass the whole thing over the seat, and let the baby take it from there.

♥   We've learned never to point out the window unless the object of interest is going to be visible for a while, or unless we're planning to pull over for a long look. Babies aren't very good at following a pointing finger!

♥   I carry a cup of cereal and raisins and, when things get rough, put some in each compartment of a seven-day pillbox. The baby likes opening the little doors to find the snacks.

♥   *"Take along a timer and set it for a [certain] period. . . .*
Tell your children that when it rings you will make the next
stop."

> —Paula Goldstein in "Traveling With the Young Child," *Long Island Parent,*
> June/July 1989.

♥   We tried to end every drive on an exciting note, even if it
meant doing a dance in the parking lot at the mall. This way,
the ride itself became a means to some sort of fun at the end.

♥   On long trips, we rotate seats—car seat and all—every
thirty minutes or so. Even the expressway looks different
from the opposite window.

♥   When we really get desperate, we give the baby an old
harmonica that we keep in the glove compartment for emergencies. Then we turn up the radio for ourselves!

11

Visits, Outings, and Errands

Anyone who's tried it can tell you that visiting, shopping, or sightseeing with a baby in tow isn't quite as easy as it looks. Special baby tactics will be needed to help you choose your destination and prepare for an outing with your infant, and to help keep both you and your older baby smiling through a visit with friends or relatives. This chapter presents the suggestions of experienced parents on dealing with the stresses of going out and about or entertaining when accompanied by your baby. Enjoy!

INFANTS (Newborn to 8 Months)

Is a lot of preparation necessary when going out with an infant?

An infant is quite "portable," some say, particularly during the first few months when loving arms, a diaper, and some liquid nourishment are all he needs to see him through a morning! But parents who try a spur-of-the moment visit, outing, or even a simple errand with their little one usually discover that some advance planning would have made for a more enjoyable time.

Even if you intend to be away from home for only an hour, a lot can happen to foil such plans once you depart. What if your infant is unusually fussy that day? What if you're invited to extend your visit or want to make an extra stop on the way home? What if you find yourself delayed by car trouble or heavy traffic? If you dashed out with only your wallet, car keys, and baby, chances are he'll be without a place to nap, enough diapers, food, and even, should the weather change, proper clothing. Add to this his inevitable overstimulation, and you'll have a problem on your hands, with none of your usual resources to help you solve it.

But going out with an infant doesn't have to result in calamity. By following a few ground rules, you and your baby will be able to rise to almost any occasion while out and about.

First, pack extra food and diapers. Then, you'll both be ready for anything. Second, ensure that your infant has been fed, rested, and changed just prior to leaving home. This practically guarantees a few extra minutes of good humor on his part. If he's under five months and fits well in a reclining stroller, you might try shopping or visiting during his naptime. And finally, remember that no matter how social your infant and no matter how often he's been to a particular place, he can still sense that it's not home. Be ready to leave at the first sign of distress (or better yet, while all is still going well) in order to avoid a hasty, shriek-accompanied scramble to gather jackets, bottles, toys, and the like before you go.

So, some preparation *is* needed for visits, outings, and errands if you wish to return home with an infant blissfully unaffected by the day's whereabouts. Since babies don't come equipped with patience, keep expectations realistic about your ventures into the public. When an outing fails miserably despite your preparations, wait a few weeks and, armed with the insight you gained the first time, try again! These tips from other parents may help you get started:

Preparing for an Outing With an Infant

♥   If we're going to a public attraction, I first consider school and day-camp schedules and then try to select a date and time when large groups won't be there.

♥   To help us make informed decisions about when to go and what to pack, we always call ahead to check on nursing, changing, and picnicking facilities, and, in summer, the existence of shade.

♥   Once he started snacking and crawling, we always made sure to dress our baby in dark, collarless clothing and brought along an extra shirt and pants to mix and match with whatever he had on.

♥   *"Bring more toys, books, bottles of juice, diapers and changes of clothes than you think would supply an entire army."*
—Mother of two Judsen Culbreth, editor-in-chief, *Working Mother* magazine.

♥   No matter where we're going, I take along a blanket, a small pail, and a four-inch plastic dump truck. If the baby needs a change of pace, she can stretch, roll, crawl, and fill her toys with acorns, rocks, or whatever small items we can find.

♥   In crowded places, we always clipped a bicycle flag on the handle of the stroller and dressed the baby in bright red.

♥   I made and laminated an identification tag listing the baby's name, age, and several phone numbers. When we go out in public, I tuck it in her pocket.

♥   We avoided many headaches by calling around for the advice of another parent who'd recently been to our intended destination.

♥   *"I pack a large variety of snacks in Ziploc bags and keep them in a small cardboard box so they won't crush."*
—Port Washington Parent Resource Center's Trudy Hoffman.

♥   We don't go unless we can be there ten minutes before opening. No matter where we're headed, we've found that this practically guarantees an hour of crowd-free sightseeing.

♥   I prepare the baby by showing her books related to where we'll be going. Once we get home, I reinforce what she's seen by using dolls or toys to reenact some part of our visit.

♥   *"Try not to bring a stroller. It's cumbersome and severely limits verbal interaction between you and your child. There are many infant carriers available which will allow you to hear each other."*
—Learning disabilities specialist Heidi Reichel in "Summer Exploration," *Long Island Parent*, June/July 1989.

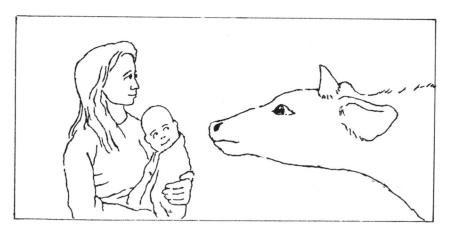

♥   I always tried to figure the total cost of an outing, right down to gas and tolls. Since a bad day on the baby's part might mean heading for home after only an hour or two, I wanted to be sure it was worth it for us to go.

♥   We attempted important excursions only in good weather because, no matter what our destination, we often needed access to the outdoors as a change of pace during long afternoons away from home. So, we always kept a plan B on the back burner in case of rain or cold.

♥   After taking my afraid-of-dogs-and-cats baby to an animal farm, only to have him scream into my collar for the duration of our visit, I learned to consider his current fears and dislikes when choosing our destination.

Outings Suited to Babies

♥   A copy of our local fire department's summer parade schedule helped us introduce our babies to the magic of marching bands.

♥   There's a pond not too far from my house where we feed the ducks, throw rocks into the water, and watch the "waterfall" created by the adjoining creek.

♥   I take my son for a leisurely stroll through a local pet store. To him, it's as exciting as a zoo!

♥   I asked our children's librarian for permission to sit with my son on the fringes of her preschoolers' storytimes. The baby is too busy taking everything in to cause any disruption.

♥   *"Choose child-friendly locations—family-style restaurants, fast-food places, sidewalk cafes. You'll feel more relaxed about dining, and you'll get more help keeping your child happy."*

—Writer and mother of two Susan Lapinski in "Table for Three, Please," *American Baby,* June 1990.

♥   We've scouted every educational toy store in the area and make frequent visits to those which have "try-out areas."

♥   My baby is fascinated by animals, so I called local nursery schools for information on zoos or farms within a reasonable distance of my home.

♥   *"Don't miss . . . beaches. [Your baby will enjoy watching you] feed the gulls, collect shells and plant life, draw designs on the wet sand using a twig. . . ."*

> —Ellyce Field and Susan Shlom in *Kids and Cars* (Melius and Peterson Publishing Corporation, 1988).

♥   We go out for an early lunch now and then. I find that if we get there before 11:30, we're sometimes treated to a look in the kitchen, or at least a stroll around the premises before things become rushed and crowded.

♥   I call the department of parks and recreation for lists of plays and concerts in our area. Even when it's not a children's program, my baby is entertained for a while by the crowds and the music.

♥   We used to grab the umbrella stroller or the front carrier and take a train ride to any station that had a park or shopping area within walking distance.

♥   *"[Get on a dozen libraries' mailing lists for information about] songfests, concerts, puppet shows, storytelling and folk instrument programs. . . ."*

> —"May Calendar of Events," *Westchester Family,* May 1990.

♥   I put my daughter in the backpack and take a walk along a nature trail. There's lots to see, touch, and smell; and she's calmed by the quiet and the change of scenery.

♥   We drive to a nearby pier where we find seagulls, boats of all shapes and sizes, and an interesting collection of people fishing and crabbing, all for my baby's entertainment.

♥ I used to call on every advertisement I could find for baby gym and Mommy-and-Me programs. Even when we had no intention of joining, we were usually invited to "Open Houses" to try out their facilities.

OLDER BABIES (9 to 15 Months)

Why do many babies now fuss, cling to you, or become wild when you deviate from routine?

Most of us suspect that our babies' adaptability to new faces and strange environments is viewed as a reflection of the kind of parents we are. But anyone who has staggered through preparation for, and a visit from, an old friend with a weepy one-year-old attached to his or her leg will rightfully insist that this kind of behavior is certainly no reflection on us adults!

The situation a baby creates when he becomes this demanding is equally hard for him. Remember that from about seven to thirteen months, the average baby needs his parents to stay close; as he learns to discriminate friends from strangers, this attachment may increase. There's probably plenty he'd rather be doing besides clinging to you; but he finds the fact that your attention has been turned elsewhere for longer than a few moments to be quite unsettling. In new surroundings, he's apt to be torn between a desire to explore and his need for you; and even in his own home, he may be afraid to roam in the presence of new faces.

Sometimes, the excitement of visiting is too much for a baby. He doesn't know what the ground rules are in this new playground, but he'll quickly figure them out from his parents' reactions as he races from place to place, touching everything in sight. At home, if parents have been preoccupied with host/hostess details, he may simply be bored. In either case, there won't be much opportunity for adult conversation until he's a bit older!

In the meantime, you can help matters by anticipating and then heading off problems. Try to confine visits to simple places where babies are welcome, tailoring the outing to his interest level whenever possible. Make sure he's physically ready for company—a hungry, uncomfortable, or tired baby won't stay contented for long. And be aware of both the baby's limits and your own when making plans. Will he stay happy in his stroller for a while? Are you able to listen to fifteen minutes of moans? And finally, just as you did in the early months, bring your visit to a close at the first sign of rebellion. Trying for a few extra minutes almost always brings out a baby's worst!

Face it, one-year-olds can't be agreeable all the time. Outbursts, clinginess, and the unstoppable urge to explore are all a normal part of their development. While you wait for the chance to hold a conversation from a seated position on the couch, or at least with your eyes on the speaker instead of on your traveling dynamo, try to remind yourself that the relationship you and your baby are building is based on all kinds of interactions—some of them embarrassingly public! Here are some ideas that may help along the way:

Planning a Visit—to You or by You—That Involves an Older Baby

♥   For now, we limit our daytime visits to Grandma's or to homes of other people with babies. There's no point in attempting a conversation in a home where babyproofing and a playroom full of toys aren't already a fact of life.

♥   I always take along a meal for my baby, regardless of what will be served. This allows me to feed him when I want to and frees me from coaxing him to "try this" or "taste that" while the rest of us eat.

♥   Before we exit the car (or, if we're the hosts, as our guests are coming up the front walk), I remind her very simply that her job is to play while the grownups visit. I don't know how much she understands, but my last-minute reminder seems to help.

♥ *"That voyage never has luck where each one has a vote."*

> —The Oxford Dictionary of English Proverbs, edited by F. P. Wilson, third
> edition (Oxford University Press, 1970).

♥ If our guests have small children, I set up a play corner with six or eight toys and hide everything else in the nursery. I find that offering access to the entire toy chest leads to fighting and a huge mess.

♥ When we visit friends who have a baby, I always take along a few of my own son's most familiar toys. Chances are, he'll ignore them while he's there, but the other baby will be distracted from the fact that *his* things are being handled by the visitor.

♥ Regardless of their outcome, *"Most trips are worth a second visit. The child usually experiences things differently every time he visits. . . ."*

> —Teacher, writer, and lecturer Pegine Herbin, mother of two, in "Trips for
> Tots," Long Island Parent, March 1989.

♥ I ask guests to come an hour before my baby's nap time. This gives them a chance to "visit" with her first and then enjoy two uninterrupted hours with us adults while the baby sleeps.

♥   As long as my baby was willing to nap away from home, we tried to schedule visits so that she'd sleep for part of them. Now that she's begun to fight this, we've moved up our arrival time so that we can get a visit in and then have her sleep on the way home.

♥   We try to combine baby and company by keeping things casual. We serve simple food and drink buffet-style from the dining room table, asking our guests to help themselves to refills, and carry on our conversations from a seat on the floor where our son can climb on us to his heart's content.

♥   If I knew the house we were visiting, I always made specific childproofing requests beforehand. This allowed us all to relax and gave the baby a bit more freedom once we got there.

♥   *"A year to a year and a half can be a frustrating time for both parent and child. Many parents prefer to stay away from stimulating unfamiliar environments . . . during this period on the borderline before language is a truly useful tool."*

> —Sanford and Joan Portnoy in How to Take Great Trips With Your Kids (Harvard Common Press, 1983).

♥   Doing as much preparation as possible the night before— vacuuming, cleaning bathrooms, hors d'oeuvres preparation, etc.—allows us to be more attentive to the baby in the hours before company comes.

♥   I have a quilted shopping-cart seat that wraps around the baby, through his legs, and around the back of a dining-room chair. We use this as a spare highchair when we entertain friends with a baby or go visiting ourselves.

♥   I take my baby's own bowl, sipper cup, and utensils wherever we dine. She likes the familiarity and I like not having to rummage through someone else's cabinets for unbreakables.

Bringing Out Baby's Best Side When Going Out or Entertaining

♥ Mid-visit, we find a reason to go outside for a few minutes. This gives us all a break from saying (or hearing) "No!" and "Don't!"

♥ I carry a book, a toy, a canteen of juice with a straw, and a package of peanut-butter-and-cheese crackers when we're out. My baby likes helping himself to a snack, and I don't have to feel guilty about waiting on lines if he's happy.

♥ *"Relax, smile and have fun. Then let the baby interact with the adults."*

—Tatum O'Neal, actress and mother of two.

♥ When eating at a restaurant, we make out best if we arrive well before the usual meal hour. 10:45 A.M. lunches and 4:45 P.M. dinners mean empty tables, faster service, and less pressure to make the baby cooperate.

♥ We're matter-of-fact about tantrums. We just pick up and leave with a casual "Time to go," rather than with embarrassment and apologies.

♥ From the beginning, we never purchased souvenirs on outings. Content to hold their usual brochure or map, it never occurred to our babies to whine for something on display.

♥ *"Create a special 'family whistle' that children will recognize if they become lost or separated in a crowd, and practice using it at home."*

—Vicki Lansky in *Traveling With Your Baby* (Bantam Books, 1985).

♥ We keep outings and visits very short. It's better to have the baby crying to stay than it is to overstay and have her crying to go home.

♥   I make sure every visit includes some fun for the baby. If she's not enjoying herself, she'll see to it that we don't, either!

♥   We make our visits to public places after 3:30. By then, school groups have left and almost everyone else is home napping babies or starting dinner.

♥   When the baby starts complaining, I can usually snap him out of it by redirecting his attention with a shout of "Hey! Look at this!" or by getting him physically involved in whatever we're doing.

♥   *"Know your own limits . . . [and] decide how far you will go to keep things running smoothly. Are you willing to buy that extra [snack]?"*

> —Parenting expert Bernice Weissbourd in "Two-Year-Olds and Public Places," *Parents*, May 1988.

♥   I discovered quite by accident that department stores are virtually empty on the second morning of a multi-day sale, yet most of the advertised items are still available. Shopping with the baby is much nicer under these conditions.

♥   I never visit a store without first phoning ahead to verify that they actually have what I'm looking for. I've saved my baby and myself many wasted trips this way.

♥   I abandoned economy for sanity by confining my shopping to a single store that carried most of what I needed, or at least to a single shopping center. The fewer trips in and out of the car seat, the better we both were.

12
Overnight Trips

Whether you're traveling for business, pleasure, or a family obligation, taking an overnight trip with a baby means that you'll be comforting and caring for her in unfamiliar surroundings. Parents of infants will need certain baby tactics as they plan, pack for, and make a long-distance journey; and parents of older babies who want to help their little ones through long days and nights away from home will need some help as well. This chapter presents the suggestions of experienced parents on solving the problems of overnight travel. Bon voyage!

INFANTS (Newborn to 8 Months)

What can you expect on a vacation trip with an infant?

Traveling and vacationing with a newborn who dozes from feeding to feeding can be a relatively uncomplicated affair. But that sixth sense that alerts her to any change in her surroundings kicks in as early as the second month, creating havoc with her eating and sleeping patterns while you're away. And since the mood of the youngest family member is likely to set the tone of the trip, it's a good idea to suit your plans to her needs.

There are many factors to consider, the first of which is your mode of travel. Besides the well-publicized ear discomfort often caused by takeoffs, air travel (and, for that matter, journeys by boat, bus, or train as well) can present quite a challenge when an infant is aboard. The resourceful parent can manage breast-, bottle-, and even spoon-feeding almost anywhere, but diaper-changing and play facilities are apt to be severely limited while en route. This is not as big a problem in the early months as it will be a bit later, when your then-wriggly little one tries to roll away during diapering and balk at spending most of the trip on your lap.

Whether your destination is a grandparent's house, a luxury hotel, or a campsite, you'll be without your usual resources once you arrive. You'll probably have to rely upon the few toys you packed for indoor entertainment, coping all the while with surroundings that are a far cry from your babyproofed home. When it comes to meal times and daily activities, you may find yourself at the mercy of your hosts or the management who often have adult guests in mind when making plans. And you'll be faced with convincing your infant to sleep in something other than the bassinet or crib she's grown used to.

Fortunately, manufacturers recognize the fact that today's young families like to keep on the go. Some travel problems can be avoided simply by shopping with your mobile lifestyle in mind. Lightweight, collapsable versions of cribs, strollers, and highchairs are widely available, and there are infant car seats that double as cradles or feeding chairs. You can buy diaper bags that fold out into beds, baby carriers that can be worn on both front and back, windscreens, clip-on umbrellas, and even infant-sized screen rooms!

A good travel agent can be just as indispensable as the right baby gear when mapping out a trip. He or she can look into baby-related services on various airlines and cruise ships and can often provide first-hand insight into facilities along the road and rails as well. In fact, barring only the unforeseen, some careful planning and thoughtful packing may be all you need to enjoy traveling with your infant. You may find some tips for your next journey among the following:

Planning and Packing for a Vacation Trip with an Infant

♥ Our easiest trips with babies were those to destinations in our time zone, thus avoiding any adjustment in feeding and sleep schedules.

♥ I made a child's plastic toolbox into a portable medicine chest and kept it in our carry-on luggage where we could get to it in a hurry.

♥ We made sure to pack our own babyproofing equipment—outlet and door-handle covers, corner guards, and lots of sturdy rubber bands for securing cabinet knobs.

♥ *"Of all the items we took on our trip, the most valuable was our willingness to laugh."*

—Toni Sands Barrass in "Have Baby, Will Travel," *American Baby,* July 1989.

♥ In case of lost luggage, one of our carry-on bags is packed with whatever we'd need to see us through the first twenty-four hours—fresh clothing, sleepwear, diapers, a receiving blanket, formula, etc.

♥ For trips longer than three days, I ask my pediatrician to provide two doctors' names and the location of the emergency room nearest our destination.

♥   We try to eliminate some of the stress of coming home by freezing two or three dinners and by stocking up on non-perishable groceries and baby supplies before we leave for our trip.

♥   It seemed to take the baby a day or two to settle into new surroundings, so we tried to make vacations worthwhile by staying away at least four days.

♥   *"This is the time to do all the traveling you can. A child this age . . . will be no more fussy in Bangkok than she would be in your own family room."*
            —Brooke Jennings Kane in "Vacations," *Parent and Child*, May/June 1990.

♥   To leave both hands free for the baby, I take along a backpack instead of a tote bag.

♥   Since rest stops along the way can leave something to be desired, I always add a half-empty roll of toilet paper, a four-ounce juice bottle, and a package of cheese and crackers to my purse.

♥   *". . . Well-nourished western children who go [to even the most underdeveloped and disease-prone countries] often resist local infections better than their parents. It is essential not to be put off by well-meaning people who think that the United States is the only safe place for [babies]."*
            —John Cobb, M.D., in *Babyshock* (Prentice Hall, Inc., 1983).

♥   Since our carry-on baggage suddenly seems to require a couple of packhorses, I now tag every bag, every piece of baby apparatus, and the baby himself with our name, phone number, and a business address.

♥   I used to pack several identical pairs of socks and booties so that if one was lost, we'd have several mates for the remaining one. Since little shirts and shorts can disappear as well, we brought along only one-piece baby outfits.

♥ Bottled water is a must for our room, as is powdered formula, baby cereal, a small bottle of laundry detergent, and clothespins.

Traveling With an Infant by Plane, Train, Boat, or Bus

♥ We make an advance visit to our port of departure. Once we're familiar with the "lay of the land," we can better plan for the day we'll actually be leaving.

♥ The journey to a friend's or relative's house is much easier when we ship the baby's spare infant seat and a few toys ahead of time.

♥ To avoid noise and crowds, we request plane seats as far as possible from the bathrooms and the galley.

♥ We considered direct, nonstop travel well worth any extra cost. The logistics involved in stopping and starting again when traveling with a baby were too stressful, no matter what the savings.

♥ Flight attendants are able to be much more attentive when the plane is half-empty; in fact, they positively fuss over the baby when we fly at off-peak times.

♥ We stick to off-peak flight times and request an aisle and a window seat. With luck, the middle seat will remain empty, because no one wants to sit between two parents juggling an infant!

♥ We carry an extra receiving blanket with us to use as a tent for the baby during naptime.

♥ When we can get bulkhead seats, we set up the umbrella stroller as a seat for the baby.

♥ *"It might be nice to catch up on paperwork or knit . . . [but] your best bet is just to concentrate on keeping your child happy."*

—Jack Gillis in "The Child-Friendly Skies," *Child*, May 1990.

♥ We try to board the train early in order to claim two bench seats which face each other. The floor space between comes in handy, as does the extra bench when the baby naps.

♥ Regardless of boarding calls for "families with small children," we prefer to spend those last few minutes before departure walking around. We board last, not first.

♥ *"Not all ships have [cribs, high chairs, and booster seats] available for your stateroom or cabin, and those that do often have limited supplies. . . . Request them when you book the cruise, and follow up when you pay and again when you board."*

—Senior Editor Christine Loomis in "Cruising: A Low-Cost Family Vacation," *Parents*, May 1989.

♥ We bring our stroller aboard on long train trips. If the baby gets fussy, we give her rides up and down the aisle.

♥ Avoiding public transportation altogether was the solution to many of my family's travel problems. Now we vacation in a rented motor home.

♥ I double-diaper the baby just before boarding and hope that he'll wet only while we're traveling. But even if a change is necessary, having the second diaper already in place makes things easier.

OLDER BABIES (9 to 15 Months)

Why does long-distance travel with an older baby require some extra resourcefulness?

There are problems inherent in any form of travel where babies are concerned; after all, little ones usually aren't the most adaptable of creatures! Most parents find, however, that travel hassles multiply as a baby approaches her first birthday.

Her physical state has just as much effect as ever on how agreeable she's feeling, but comfortable travel clothing, moderate temperatures, and a security blanket may no longer be enough. The fact that babies predisposed to motion sickness often begin feeling its effects by twelve months adds a new element to trips of any kind, for parents must now incorporate such things as full stomachs, highway driving, and overnight travel into their planning.

You must also consider that by nine months, a baby is awake and aware for a good part of the day. As such, she is very much affected by changes in her surroundings and may experience fear, overstimulation, or a simple unwillingness to sleep while away from home. She's also quite mobile by now and won't take kindly to the physical restrictions incurred aboard a ship or by your cousin's living room full of antiques! The fact that you'll be working harder than usual to keep her happy may defeat the purpose of getting away in the first place, so try to be realistic when deciding on your destination, mode of travel, and length of stay.

As a growing baby really begins to make her presence known, parents must attune themselves more than ever to their hosts' and other guests' noise and mess thresholds. You may not be much help around the house while your baby is awake, nor will you be able to convince the little one to play quietly for the trip's duration, but there are still plenty of ways to be considerate! Sweep up the cornflakes scattered under the dining room table, take complete charge of diaper disposal, keep baby's toys confined to one corner, and get her out of the house once a day to give others some peace.

It's often helpful to stick closely to your ordinary routine when away from home. If you are visiting, you can approach your hosts well in advance about such things as babyproofing, sleep and meal arrangements, and itineraries. If your lodgings are private, don't be afraid to take a simple meal in your room or to spend a quiet afternoon by the kiddie pool. A good rule of thumb is to plan *less* than you think your family can handle; rushing and scheduling may prove costly to your baby's good humor!

In the end, your aim while traveling should be to relax as much as possible. These ideas may help you look back on your next trip with a smile rather than a shudder:

Helping a Baby Through Days Away From Home

♥   I prepare myself at the outset to spend much more time entertaining the baby than I would have to if we were at home. If I don't look forward to leisure time, then every bit that I do get is a treat.

♥   Rather than assume our hosts will have activities planned for us each day, I do a little research ahead of time to ensure that we won't just be hanging around their living room.

♥   If we're planning an afternoon activity, we take it slow in the morning, ordering a room-service breakfast and strolling the grounds of the hotel. If we're up and out early, we devote the afternoon to naps, quiet play, and a low-key dinner.

♥   We avoided stress by eating as many meals as possible in the room or in the car. We packed lots of jarred baby foods and used the motel coffee shop and nearby fast-food places for take-out breakfasts and dinners.

♥   We never stayed in friends' homes if one of our children was under age three. Visits were much easier on everyone if we stayed in a nearby motel.

♥   With our hosts' permission, we raid their cabinets for entertaining items once any toys we've brought along have lost their appeal.

♥   If the people we're staying with have children, there's always the fear of inappropriate toys finding their way into the baby's hands. Restricting her to a single play area helps us relax and also eliminates the worry that she's trashing the house.

♥   *"Instead of a whirlwind tour, choose central locations, and plan day trips from there. Your baby feels more secure coming home to a familiar room. . . ."*

> —Valerie Sager Phillips in "Up, Up and Away," *American Baby,* June 1988.

♥   To keep some order in our room while still giving the baby access to his toys, we scrub out one of the wastebaskets in the room, line it with a towel, and use it as a toy chest.

♥   We used to wrack our brains for baby activities we could oversee without actually having to join in. Water play on our balcony, the sandbox, or a new toy from the gift shop usually worked for us.

♥   *"There are two 'best ages' [to vacation with children]: one when the oldest child is 6 weeks old and will spend the entire trip sleeping and the other when the youngest child is 33. . . . Any age in between is a bust."*

> —Teresa Bloomingdale in *I Should Have Seen it Coming When the Rabbit Died* (Doubleday and Co., 1979).

♥   *"Friends who have traveled to different places with their families can be especially helpful. Ask them to describe. . . what they did. . . . Listen for general ideas about places to check out."*

> —Sanford and Joan Portnoy in *How To Take Great Trips With Your Kids* (Harvard Common Press, 1983).

♥   After we check in, I walk the baby up and down the corridor pointing to all the closed doors, saying "Shhhhh—everybody's sleeping!" I say the same words each time we exit our room and again whenever she becomes too noisy in the room.

♥   One parent goes early to the restaurant and orders for all three of us. The other parent and the baby arrive fifteen minutes later—fifteen minutes that would have been spent trying to keep him happy in a strange high-chair.

♥   By buying some nonperishable foods like granola bars, bread, peanut butter, juice boxes, and cheese-crackers for our room, we were able to bring bag lunches (which wouldn't bankrupt us and which the baby would actually *eat*) wherever we went.

Helping a Baby to Sleep Away From Home

♥   We bring along a cool-mist vaporizer to provide "white noise" during the night.

♥   On vacations, our babies always set the bedtime for the whole family. With the room dark and everyone settled down, no one had a problem going off to sleep.

♥   *"Stay long enough to settle in. . . . Everyone may be restless the first few nights in an unfamiliar bed, but the third and fourth nights are much better."*

> —Ellyce Field and Susan Shlom in *Kids and Cars* (Melius and Peterson Publishing, Inc., 1988).

♥　　We spend a lot of time in the room the first day, coming in and going out as many times as possible. The more homey it feels by nighttime, the more likely the baby is to go to sleep without a tussle.

♥　　I try to duplicate his own crib by taking along the bumpers, sheets, and blankets that he uses at home. He's apt to sleep better in a bed that smells and feels familiar.

♥　　We roll the crib against the window and, after nightfall, pull the drapes around it to block out the light from the rest of the room.

♥　　*"Pack a night-light [and] rubber sheet for the mattress in case of 'accidents'. . . ."*

　　　—Anne Munoz-Furlong in "The Family Travel Companion," *American Baby,*
　　　July 1990.

♥　　We never bothered with a strange crib. Our babies slept in a double bed with a parent on one side and the wall or a line of chair backs on the other.

♥　　Splurging on a two-room suite solved our bedtime problems. Even in strange surroundings, my daughter would fall asleep in minutes as long as she couldn't see or hear the two of us.

♥　　I break all my usual rules when we're traveling, putting an exhausted baby, already asleep, to bed at 10:00 P.M. We never hear from her until morning.

♥　　We make sure to schedule a nap and at least two hours of late-afternoon unwinding time. Otherwise, she's too strung out to sleep well by bedtime.

♥　　*"Be prepared to take extra time to get your child to sleep. Sometimes it's necessary to turn off the light and wait outside in the hall. . . ."*

　　　—Vicki Lansky in *Traveling With Your Baby* (Bantam Books, 1985).

♥   When the baby woke up and was frightened by his strange surroundings, I took him into the dark bathroom and switched on the exhaust fan. The sound lulled him back to sleep and prevented his cries from disturbing anyone else.

♥   I used to take my son on my lap, wrap him in a heavy blanket, dim the lights, and play the TV very softly. In ten or fifteen minutes, he'd be out like a light.

♥   We avoid middle-of-the-night screams by keeping the room pitch black. If the baby can't see where she is, she forgets she's away from home.

"Where did everybody go?"

Conclusion

When all is said and done, you, the parent, are your child's decision-maker. No child-rearing professional will ever know your baby's likes, dislikes, fascinations, and fears the way you will through the intimacy of day-to-day, round-the-clock living. In fact, a few months of on-the-job experience will likely render *you* just as much the parenting expert. And as such, it's up to you to sort through the baby-care information and advice that abounds in today's world, and apply that which you feel is best suited to your baby and your situation.

If there's a single baby tactic that should be universally adapted by today's busy mothers and fathers, it is this suggestion by Wyckoff Heights Medical Center's Alvin N. Eden, M.D., chairman and director, department of pediatrics:

Find the time every single day to remind your child how happy you are to be his or her parent. It is never too early to start building up the baby's self-esteem.

Happy parenting!

Readers' Suggestions

If you have a baby tactic that you'd care to pass along to other parents, please send it to us for future editions of this book. Send your idea, along with your name, address, occupation, and baby's age to:

Barbara Albers Hill
c/o Avery Publishing Group
120 Old Broadway
Garden City Park, NY 11040

Submitting your suggestion constitutes your permission for its use. Thank you for sharing your parenting expertise!

Resources

American Baby magazine, Cahners Publishing Co., Newton, MA.

American Baby's *Healthy Kids: Birth-3* series, Cahners Publishing Co, Newton, MA.

Baby and Child Care, Benjamin Spock, M.D., Pocket Books, New York, N.Y., 1976.

Baby Talk magazine, Parenting Unlimited, Inc., New York, N.Y.

Babyshock, John Cobb, M.D., Prentice-Hall, New York, N.Y., 1983.

Best Bets for Babies, Brooke McKamy Beebe, Dell Publishing Co., New York, N.Y., 1985.

Bringing Out the Best in Your Baby, Art Ulene, M.D., Mac-Millan Publishing Co., New York, N.Y., 1986.

Child magazine, New York Times Magazine Group, New York, N.Y.

Curing Infant Colic, Bruce Taubman, M.D., Bantam Books, New York, N.Y., 1990.

Dr. Green's Baby Book, Dr. Christopher Green, Fawcett Columbine, New York, N.Y., 1988.

The First Three Years of Life, Burton L. White, Prentice-Hall, New York, N.Y., 1975.

How to Take Great Trips With Your Kids, Sanford and Joan Portnoy, Harvard Common Press, Boston, MA, 1983.

Kids and Cars, Ellyce Field and Susan Shlom, Melius and Peterson Publishing Corp., Aberdeen, SD, 1988.

Parenting magazine, Time Publishing Ventures, San Francisco, CA.

Parents *Baby Care* series, Gruner and Jahr USA Publishing, New York, N.Y.

Parents magazine, Gruner and Jahr USA Publishing, New York, N.Y.

The Self-Calmed Baby: A Revolutionary New Approach to Parenting Your Infant, William A. H. Sammons, M.D., Little, Brown and Co., Boston, MA, 1989.

79 Ways to Calm a Crying Baby, Diana S. Greene, Pocket Books, New York, N.Y., 1989.

Silent Nights for You and Your Baby, Jane Asher, Dell Publishing Co., New York, N.Y., 1984.

Stopping Baby's Colic, Ted Ayllon, Ph.D., Perigee Books, New York, N.Y., 1989.

Traveling With Your Baby, Vicki Lansky, Bantam Books, New York, N.Y., 1985.

What Every Baby Knows, T. Berry Brazelton, M.D., Addison-Wesley Publishing Co., Reading, MA, 1987.

Working Mother magazine, Working Woman/McCall's Group, New York, N.Y.

Your Baby and Child, Penelope Leach, Ph.D., Alfred A. Knopf, Inc., New York, N.Y., 1989.

Your Child at Play, Marilyn Segal, Ph.D. and Don Adcock, Ph.D., Newmarket Press, New York, N.Y., 1985.

Your Newborn Baby, Michael Krauss, Warner Books, New York, N.Y., 1988.

PERMISSION CREDITS

The following credits are for use of copyrighted material in this book. They have been used with permission of:

Chapter 1

Michael Krauss, *Your Newborn Baby*, Warner Books, 1988.

Diana S. Greene, *79 Ways to Calm a Crying Baby*, copyright © 1989, Pocket Books, a division of Simon and Schuster, Inc.

Ted Ayllon, Ph.D., *Stopping Baby's Colic*, copyright © 1989, Perigee Books.

William A.H. Sammons, M.D., *The Self-Calmed Baby: A Revolutionary New Approach to Parenting Your Infant*, Little, Brown and Co., 1989.

Shirley Leuth, *Bubble, Bubble, Toil and Trouble*, William Morrow and Co., 1984.

Bartlett's Familiar Quotations, Little, Brown and Co., 1980.

Janice T. Gibson, Ed.D., *Parents*, October 1988.

Silent Nights for You and Your Baby, copyright © 1987 by Jane Asher, Dell Publishing Company, a division of Bantam, Doubleday, Dell Publishing Group, Inc.

Penelope Leach, *Your Baby and Child*, Alfred A. Knopf, Inc., 1989.

Dr. Benjamin Spock, *Baby and Child Care*, copyright © 1945, 46, 57, 68, 76. Reprinted by permission of Pocket Books, a division of Simon and Schuster, Inc.

Chapter 2

Bruce Taubman, M.D., *Infant Colic*, Bantam Books, 1990.

Dr. Christopher Green, *Dr. Green's Baby Book*, Fawcett Columbine, 1988.

William A.H. Sammons, M.D., *The Self-Calmed Baby: A Revolutionary New Approach to Parenting Your Infant*, Little, Brown and Co., 1989.

Sandy Jones, "Crying and Colic," reprinted with permission from American Baby's *Healthy Kids: Birth-3*, Spring/Summer 1990, copyright © 1990, Reed Publishing USA.

Eleanore Duse, *2500 Anecdotes for All Occasions*, Edmund Fuller, Ed., Avenel Books, Crown Publishing Group, 1980.

Diana S. Greene, *79 Ways to Calm a Crying Baby*, Pocket Books, a division of Simon and Schuster, Inc., 1989.

Poor Richard's Almanack, Hallmark Editions, 1967.

T. Berry Brazelton, M.D., *What Every Baby Knows*, copyright © 1987, reprinted by permission of Addison-Wesley Publishing Co., Inc., Reading, MA.

Chapter 3

Michael Krauss, *Your Newborn Baby,* Warner Books, 1988.

The First Year of Life, copyright © 1987, Cahners Publishing Co., a division of Reed Publishing USA.

Ellen J. Sackoff, "Dressing Your Baby," *Baby Talk,* April 1990.

Nancy Issing, R.N., A.C.C.E., "Squeaky Clean," *Baby Talk,* May 1990.

Marti Attoun, *Joplin Globe.*

Dr. Benjamin Spock, *Baby and Child Care,* copyright © 1945, 46, 57, 68, 76, reprinted by permission of Pocket Books, a division of Simon and Schuster, Inc.

"Kidfile: On Becoming a Toddler," *Parenting* magazine, April 1990.

Joyce Maynard, *Domestic Affairs: Enduring the Pleasures of Motherhood and Family Life,* Times Books, copyright © 1987.

Teresa Bloomingdale, *I Should Have Seen It Coming When the Rabbit Died,* Doubleday and Co., 1979.

Chapter 4

Breastfeeding: The Best Start for Your Baby, February 1989, provided courtesy of Mead-Johnson Nutritional Group.

The Oxford Dictionary of English Proverbs, edited by F.P. Wilson, third edition, 1970 (Oxford University Press).

Beech-Nut Stages Guide to Infant Feeding, copyright © 1985, reprinted with permission of Beech-Nut Nutrition Corporation.

Jean Kerr, *How I Got To Be Perfect,* Doubleday and Co., 1978.

Poor Richard's Almanack, Hallmark Editions, 1967.

Dr. Lawrence Balter, author of *Who's in Control? Dr. Balter's Guide to Discipline Without Combat,* Poseidon/Simon & Schuster, 1989, in "Eating Behaviors," *Sesame Street Parents' Guide,* November 1989.

Mary Anne Moore, "Turning the Table on Finicky Eaters," *Parenting* magazine, September 1989.

Dr. Benjamin Spock, *Baby and Child Care,* copyright © 1945, 46, 57, 68, 76, reprinted by permission of Pocket Books, a division of Simon and Schuster, Inc.

National Live Stock and Meat Board's *A Good Guide for the First Five Years,* 1991.

Chapter 5

"Kidfile: On Becoming a Toddler," *Parenting,* April 1990.

Robert M. McCall, Ph.D., "Baby Talk," *Pampers Baby Care, 6-9 Months,* Gruner and Jahr, 1987.

Dr. T. Berry Brazelton, *What Every Baby Knows*, copyright © 1987, reprinted by permission of Addison-Wesley Publishing Co., Inc., Reading, MA.

Dr. Janine Levy, *You and Your Toddler: Sharing the Developmental Years*, copyright © 1972 by Editions du Seuil, English translation copyright © 1973 by William Collins Sons and Company Ltd., copyright © 1975 by Random House.

Burton L. White, Ph.D., *The First Three Years of Life*, copyright © 1975, reprinted by permission of Prentice Hall, a division of Simon and Schuster, Englewood Cliffs, NJ.

Jan Hart Sousa, "A Child-Proof Home," *Parents Baby Care, 9-12 Months*, Gruner and Jahr USA Publishing, 1987.

Burton Stevenson, Ed., *The Home Book of Bible Quotations*, Harper and Brothers, 1949.

Chapter 6

Denise Schipani, "The New Kid in Town," *Child*, April 1990.

Arlene Eisenberg, et al., "When Firstborn meets Newborn," *Working Mother*, June 1989. From *What to Expect in the First Year*, copyright © 1989 by Arlene Eisenberg, Heidi Eisenberg Murkoff, and Sandee Eisenberg Hathaway. Reprinted by permission of Workman Publishing Company Inc. All rights reserved.

Jean Kerr, *How I Got To Be Perfect*, Doubleday and Co., 1978.

Leonard S. Marcus, "Sibling Library," *Parenting* magazine, June/July 1989.

Lilian G. Katz, Ph.D., "Making Friends," Parents, November 1987, copyright © 1987 Gruner and Jahr USA Publishing. Reprinted from Parents magazine by permission.

Joan Shapiro, Ph.D., "She's Just Shy," from American Baby's *Healthy Kids Birth-3*, Spring/Summer 1990, copyright © 1990, Reed Publishing USA.

Ruth Mason, "First Friends," *Parents*, October 1990.

The Oxford Dictionary of English Proverbs, edited by F.P. Wilson, third edition, 1970 (Oxford University Press).

Sandra Wolkoff, C.S.W., Director of the Early Childhood Training Institute at North Shore Child and Family Guidance Center, in Neala Schwartzberg, Ph.D.'s "Teaching Your Child How to Fight the Good Fight," *Child*, January/February 1990.

From Marilyn Segal and Don Adcock's *Your Child at Play: One to Two Years*, copyright © 1985 by Marilyn Segal, Ph.D., and Don Adcock, Ph.D. Reprinted by permission of Newmarket Press, 18 East 48 Street, New York, NY 10017.

Chapter 7

Alvin Rosenfeld, M.D., and Dorothy Levine, M.D., in "Parenting Q & A," *American Baby*, June 1990, copyright © 1990 Cahners Publishing Company, a division of Reed Publishing USA.

Jean Callahan, "Who's Running the Show?" *Parenting* magazine, June/July 1990.

Louise Bates Ames, et al., *Your One Year Old*, Delacorte Press, 1982.

Christopher Green, M.D., *Dr. Green's Baby Book*, Fawcett Columbine, 1988.

The Oxford Dictionary of English Proverbs, edited by F.P. Wilson, third edition, 1970 (Oxford University Press).

Bernice Weissbourd, "Encouraging Independence," *Parents*, May 1988, copyright © 1988 Gruner and Jahr USA Publishing. Reprinted from *Parents* magazine by permission.

When Your Child is Difficult, copyright © 1980 Ross Laboratories, reprinted with permission of Ross Laboratories, Columbus, OH 43216.

Jean Kerr, *How I Got To Be Perfect,* Doubleday and Co., 1978.

Poor Richard's Almanack, Hallmark Editions, 1967.

Chapter 8

John J. Fisher, "Your Baby's First Playground," *Baby Talk*, February 1989.

Art Ulene, M.D. and Steven Shelov, M.D., *Bringing Out the Best in Your Baby,* copyright © 1986 by Feeling Fine Programs, Inc., reprinted with permission of MacMillan Publishing Company.

Ingrid Groller, "And Baby Makes Six," *Parents*, November 1988, copyright © 1988 Gruner and Jahr USA Publishing. Reprinted from *Parents* magazine by permission.

Richard A. Weinberg, Ph.D., "Choosing the Right Toys for Your Child," *Baby Talk,* October 1988.

Dr. Benjamin Spock, *Baby and Child Care*, copyright © 1945, 46, 57, 68, 76, reprinted by permission of Pocket Books, a division of Simon and Schuster, Inc.

Margaret L. Agoglia, "What's So Funny?" *Baby Talk,* February 1990.

Penelope Leach, *Your Baby and Child*, Alfred A. Knopf, 1989.

Best Bets for Babies, copyright © 1981 by Brooke McKamy Beebe, Dell Publishing Company, a division of Bantam, Doubleday, Dell Publishing Group, Inc.

Burton L. White, *The First Three Years of Life*, copyright © 1975, reprinted by permission of Prentice Hall, a division of Simon and Schuster, Englewood Cliffs, NJ.

Chapter 9

Nancy Balaban, Ed.D., "Goodbyes Without Tears," *Working Mother*, January 1989.

Best Bets for Babies, copyright © 1981 by Brooke McKamy Beebe, Dell Publishing, a division of Bantam, Doubleday, Dell Publishing Group, Inc.

Phyllis LaFarge, "A Family Day-Care Checklist," *Parents*, January 1990.

Christopher Green, M.D., *Dr. Green's Baby Book*, Fawcett Columbine, 1988.

Dr. T. Berry Brazelton, *What Every Baby Knows*, copyright © 1987, reprinted by permission of Addison-Wesley Publishing Co., Reading, MA.

Chapter 10

Vicki Lansky, *Traveling With Your Baby*, Bantam Books, 1985.

Jody Gaylin, "Car Trip Survival Guide," *Parents*, May 1990.

John Cobb, M.D., *Babyshock*, copyright © 1983, reprinted by permission of Prentice Hall, a division of Simon and Schuster, Englewood Cliffs, NJ.

Ellyce Field and Susan Shlom, *Kids and Cars*, Melius & Peterson Publishing Corporation, 1988.

Sanford and Joan Portnoy, *How to Take Great Trips With Your Kids*, copyright © 1983 by Sanford Portnoy and Joan Flynn Portnoy, reprinted with permission from the Harvard Common Press.

Toni Sands Barrass, "Have Baby, Will Travel," *American Baby*, July 1989, copyright © 1989 Cahners Publishing Company, a division of Reed Publishing USA.

Linda Lague, "Driving Controls," Good Housekeeping & Sesame Street Magazine's *Kids of Summer 1990*.

Rhonda Barfield, "The Art of Weekend Visiting," *Baby Talk*, November 1989.

Paula Goldstein, "Traveling With the Young Child," *Long Island Parent*, June/July 1989.

Chapter 11

Heidi Reichel, "Summer Exploration," *Long Island Parent*, June/July 1989.

Susan Lapinski, "Table for Three, Please," *American Baby*, June 1990, copyright © 1990 Cahners Publishing Company, a division of Reed Publishing USA.

Ellyce Field and Susan Shlom, *Kids and Cars*, Melius and Peterson Publishing Corporation, 1988.

"May Calendar of Events," *Westchester Family*, May 1990.

The Oxford Dictionary of English Proverbs, edited by F.P. Wilson, third edition, 1970 (Oxford University Press).

Pegine Herbin, "Trips for Tots," *Long Island Parent*, March 1989.

Sanford and Joan Portnoy, *How to Take Great Trips With Your Kids*, copyright © 1983 by Sanford Portnoy and Joan Flynn Portnoy, reprinted with permission from the Harvard Common Press.

Vicki Lansky, *Traveling With Your Baby*, Bantam Books, 1985.

Bernice Weissbourd, "Two-Year-Olds and Public Places," *Parents*, May 1988, copyright © 1988 Gruner and Jahr USA Publishing. Reprinted from *Parents* magazine by permission.

Chapter 12

Toni Sands Barrass, "Have Baby, Will Travel," *American Baby*, July 1989, copyright © 1989 Cahners Publishing Company, a division of Reed Publishing USA.

Brooke Jennings Kane, "Vacations," *Parent and Child,* May/June 1990.

John Cobb, M.D., *Babyshock,* copyright © 1983, reprinted by permission of Prentice Hall, a division of Simon and Schuster, Englewood Cliffs, NJ.

"The Child-Friendly Skies," *Child*, copyright © 1990 by Jack Gillis and Mary Ellen R. Fise, reprinted by permission of Sterling Lord Literistic, Inc.

Christine Loomis, "Cruising: A Low-Cost Family Vacation," *Parents*, May 1989, copyright © 1989 Gruner and Jahr USA Publishing. Reprinted from *Parents* magazine by permission.

Teresa Bloomingdale, *I Should Have Seen It Coming When the Rabbit Died,* Doubleday and Co., 1979.

Sanford and Joan Portnoy, *How to Take Great Trips With Your Kids*, copyright © 1983 by Sanford Portnoy and Joan Flynn Portnoy, reprinted with permission from Harvard Common Press.

Ellyce Field and Susan Shlom, *Kids and Cars*, Melius and Peterson Publishing, Inc., 1988.

Valerie Sager Phillips, "Up, Up and Away," *American Baby*, June 1988, copyright © 1988 Cahners Publishing Company, a division of Reed Publishing USA.

Anne Munoz-Furlong, a freelance writer specializing in issues of parenting and food allergies, "The Family Travel Companion," *American Baby,* July 1990, copyright © 1990 Cahners Publishing Company, a division of Reed Publishing USA.

Vicki Lansky, *Traveling With Your Baby*, Bantam Books, 1985.